No Child Left Behind

and the Public Schools

No Child Left Behind
and the Public Schools

Scott Franklin Abernathy

THE UNIVERSITY OF MICHIGAN PRESS
ANN ARBOR

For my parents

In memory of Annette

Copyright © by the University of Michigan 2007
All rights reserved
Published in the United States of America by
The University of Michigan Press
Manufactured in the United States of America
Printed on acid-free paper

2010   2009   2008   2007   4   3   2   1

A CIP catalog record for this book is available from the British Library.

Library of Congress Cataloging-in-Publication Data

Abernathy, Scott Franklin, 1966–
    No child left behind and the public schools / Scott Franklin
Abernathy.
        p.   cm.
    Includes bibliographical references and index.
    ISBN-13: 978-0-472-09979-5 (cloth : alk. paper)
    ISBN-10: 0-472-09979-5 (cloth : alk. paper)
    ISBN-13: 978-0-472-06979-8 (pbk. : alk. paper)
    ISBN-10: 0-472-06979-9 (pbk. : alk. paper)
        1. Educational accountability—United States.   2. Education—
Standards—United States.   3. Public schools—United States.
4. Federal aid to education—United States.   5. United States. No Child
Left Behind Act of 2001.   I. Title.
    LB2806.22.A18   2007
    379.1'580973—dc22   2006028158

Contents

Preface

Some time ago—in the eighth grade, I believe—I came to a sort of epiphany about U.S. politics. Reflecting on "I'm Just a Bill" from the *America Rock* Saturday morning educational series on ABC, I decided (for the purpose of realism) that Bill, our cartoon legislative friend trying to become a law, should be surrounded by ninety or so expired comrades scattered about on the steps of Capitol Hill. Too disturbing for little kids, of course, but a more accurate picture of the odds against success for any aspiring laws. In the world of public policy, the scene would be a little different but still a little scary. If, based on what I know now, I were to create a cartoon policy character—Polly might be a good name—I might place her instead among a collection of weird mutant policies, transformed in the process of their implementation from friendly and optimistic companions into a strange an unfortunate mélange of good intentions gone terribly wrong.

This book is about one such public policy. Its longevity and mutations have yet to be determined, but its ambitions are clear and sweeping. No Child Left Behind, signed into law by President George W. Bush in early 2002, was anything but a little bill—at nearly seven hundred pages long—and it is shaping up to be a very big policy indeed. The law promises to close the long-standing achievement gap between advantaged and disadvantaged students in the United

States by using the results of standardized tests to identify, threaten, and, if necessary, sanction schools and districts that do not fulfill this promise. Like many other policies, this one is full of complications, contradictions, and challenges.

The central complication is that success in school has a great deal to do with being luckily born—into a family that values education and has the means to support its pursuit; into potential peer groups that reinforce the path to achievement; and into well-run, well-funded, and safe schools. There is also an inherent contradiction in applying the radically centralizing reforms of No Child Left Behind and the radically decentralizing reforms of giving parents more choices in education at the same time and without much thought about the potential synergies, conflict, and confusion that might result from this unusual combination. Finally, there is always the challenge of measuring something as fleeting and contextual as "good" schooling with any objective tools, no matter how well designed. In this book, I will deal with all of these issues in some detail.

While working for three years as a public school teacher, I learned two things. First, three years is only enough time to begin to understand how complicated schools and schooling really are. Second, those who would fix schools from above and from afar rarely take into account this complex reality.

My primary goal in this book is to explore the possibility of combining the on-the-ground understandings of schooling with the power and leverage of national and state policies. This combination of street- and elite-level approaches is not tried as often as it should be, which is unfortunate. By bringing them together, I argue that we can make it much more likely that the ultimate form of No Child Left Behind will resemble something close to what we had originally hoped for it—and something not too scary, at that.

In many ways, this book began on the third floor of Robertson Hall at Princeton University. There, in the coffee break room, Professor John J. DiIulio Jr. agreed to supervise me in an independent study on the American bureaucracy. It was just John and me, along with his peripatetic chalkboard analysis of Chester Barnard, James Q. Wilson, bureaucratic agency, the problem of supervision, and the question of exactly when an organization is born. Down the hall was the office of my eventual dissertation adviser and friend, R. Douglas Arnold. I owe a great deal to both of these individuals. John, Doug, and all of the other scholars who have contributed to this book and to my education bear no responsibility for its arguments. All errors are mine and mine alone. They do, however, bear some nontrivial responsibility for instilling in me the beliefs that organizations matter, that rules matter, and that a useful path to understanding U.S. politics can begin with a study of the little details and unspoken assumptions that are often overlooked in the grand sweep of things.

Many scholars have provided invaluable comments and insight on early drafts of this work. For their comments and suggestions, I thank Larry M. Bartels, Sanford Gordon, Jacob Hacker, Jeffrey Henig, Jennifer L. Hochschild, Gregory Huber, Paul Manna, Rick Mayes, Christine Roch, Andrew Rotherham, Mark Schneider, Kevin Smith, Clarence Stone, and Paul Teske, along with anonymous reviewers of the manuscript. At the University of Minnesota, I am indebted to Teri Caraway, James Farr, Christopher Federico, Bill Flanigan, John Freeman, Lawrence Jacobs, Timothy Johnson, Daniel Kelliher, Joanne Miller, Kathryn Pearson, Wendy Rahn, Jason Roberts, Martin Sampson, Katherine Sikkink, Paul Soper, Dara Strolovich, and John Sullivan for their comments, suggestions, and support. I also thank Alexis Cuttance, Judy Iverson, Rose Miskowiec, Judith Mitchell, and Cheryl Olson for their invaluable assistance.

This project was completed with funding through a grant from the University of Minnesota's Center for Urban and Regional Affairs Faculty Interactive Research Program, and I thank Tom Scott, Will Craig, and CURA's staff for their invaluable assistance. I also thank the Office of the Dean of the Graduate School and the College of Liberal Arts of the University of Minnesota for research support for this project. I thank Robert J. Schmidt, executive director of the Minnesota Association of Secondary School Principals, and P. Fred Storti, executive director of the Minnesota Elementary School Principals' Association. In addition, I am indebted to Rossana Armson, Pam Jones, and Marc Wagoner from the Minnesota Center for Survey Research.

This project would not have been possible without the generosity of Minnesota's public and charter school principals, who provided candid and thoughtful responses to my questions. I also thank individuals from the communications departments at the Minnesota Department of Education and the Minneapolis Public Schools as well as Jim Reische, Amy Fuller, and the staff of the University of Michigan Press for all of their help and assistance. I owe a great deal to Jim for taking a chance on a revised dissertation and for being willing to work with me on a second book project anyway. And to the Replacements for "Skyway."

Mostly, I thank Sara, my wife and my best friend. In terms of effort, commitment, and survival, this book is hers as much as it is mine.

Minneapolis
June 2006

CHAPTER 1

The Best-Laid Plans

And what is good, Phaedrus, and what is not good—
need we ask anyone to tell us these things?
Robert Pirsig, paraphrasing Plato's The Phaedrus

It seemed like a good idea at the time. Samuel W. King, the newly appointed superintendent of the Portland, Oregon, schools, wanted results. Eager to improve his town's public education, King turned to standardized tests. He initiated a comprehensive system of test-based accountability, publishing the test results in the local newspapers alongside the names of the individual students, teachers, and schools. Uniform and administered annually, these tests were designed to determine student promotion and to serve as the basis for evaluations of teacher competency.

And so, in 1874, King administered the first round of his tests to Portland Oregon's fifty-four high school students.[1] Only eleven passed. King's policy of publicizing test results drew immediate opposition from parents as well as teachers. The superintendent, however, stood by his tests. "Next to a New England climate," he wrote, "these examinations necessitate industry, foster promptness and encourage pupils to do the right thing *at the right time*."[2]

The rest of the community did not agree, and a coalition of teachers and parents "forced King's resignation in 1877."[3] His successor,

Thomas Crawford, was quick to backtrack on his predecessor's reforms, keeping the test results from public consumption and criticizing their influence on the school, students, and curriculum. "It is not the excitement that is the source of much anxiety to the school authorities," Crawford argued, "but the useless and almost criminal squandering of precious time."[4] King's plan had other unintended consequences as well. The competitive spirit unleashed by these tests, according to the plan's detractors, had done "incalculable injury . . . both to the teachers and to the pupils of our free schools, resulting from a spirit of rivalry on the part of the teachers."[5] The incentive structure induced by the high-stakes nature of the program produced some highly undesirable bureaucratic behaviors, such as teachers encouraging suspensions of lower-performing students so that they would not drag down classroom averages.

We have traveled down the accountability road in education many times since King's experiment, and we have often learned—or failed to learn—the same lessons. Accurate, workable systems of test-based accountability are very hard to create and implement. They often produce apparent gains at first, but test scores inevitably reach a stubborn plateau. Testing often produces all sorts of unwanted and unforeseen changes in the behaviors of those in the school system. And they are usually abandoned or watered down in the face of organized opposition by those who stand to lose from their implementation.

This time, it might be different. Or it might not.

The No Child Left Behind Act of 2001 (NCLB), signed into law by President George W. Bush in January 2002, is at once more ambitious, more sweeping, and more consequential than any previous accountability initiative in American education. If properly implemented and sufficiently funded, NCLB holds the promise of being one of the great liberal reforms in the history of U.S. education.[6] This may sound surprising, given that the measure was passed under a Republican administration, but it is—or can be—true. The reason lies in the goals. Desegregation and the Americans with Disabilities Act were both about equality of opportunity; No Child Left Behind aims to provide equality of outcomes.[7] This is a very radical and ambitious goal. No longer content to provide access to education for traditionally excluded student populations, we are now demanding that these students receive equally good educations. In other words, we are now demanding equality of quality.

To reach this goal, No Child Left Behind places significant responsibilities on state educational agencies, school districts, principals, and teachers. It is high-stakes accountability with teeth, offering consequences for failing schools much more significant than public praise or embarrassment. Unfortunately, we have placed these liberal hopes on a large and powerful ship that is heading the wrong way.

My evidence suggests that any confidence placed in No Child Left Behind is probably misplaced. Its promise to close the achievement gap between the advantaged and the disadvantaged will go unfulfilled unless the law is significantly rethought and revised. The source of the problem lies in a failure to consider that the interface between the mind of the student and product of the school is a very difficult thing to observe and measure and may in fact be unmeasurable with complete certainty.

Unless reworked, NCLB will probably not close the achievement gap because it was not set up to distinguish between good and bad schools serving disadvantaged student populations. A fundamental reassessment of how we measure quality in education will be required to achieve the critical liberal purposes of No Child Left Behind and to avoid at least some of the unintended bureaucratic consequences that have plagued such initiatives in the past. NCLB can achieve these larger goals *if* we can get accountability right. My purpose in this book is to contribute to the exploration of *how* we can get accountability right.

How No Child Left Behind Is Supposed to Work

At 670 pages long, and with many of its key provisions modifying parts of other laws, No Child Left Behind is as large and ponderous as it is ambitious. However, two basic goals define the law. The first is "closing the achievement gap between high- and low-performing children, especially the achievement gaps between minority and non-minority students, and between disadvantaged children and their more advantaged peers."[8] It is not yet clear that the recent wave of test-based accountability is closing this gap, as researchers have found the difference in test score outcomes "stagnating or rising in the 1990's,"[9] a period of increased reliance on standards and account-ability.

The second goal of No Child Left Behind is to create and imple-ment an assessment regime with significant consequences for those who fail by "holding schools, local educational agencies, and States accountable for improving the academic achievement of all stu-dents."[10] These accountability systems, however, are subservient to the primary objective of closing the achievement gap: "The purpose of this title is to ensure that all children have a fair, equal, and significant opportunity to obtain a high quality education and reach, at a minimum, proficiency on challenging State academic achieve-ment standards and state academic assessments."[11]

Because the U.S. Constitution, unlike the state constitutions, con-tains no provision for or guarantee of an education, the federal gov-ernment can directly order a state or its public schools only to do (or not do) very little.[12] Instead, the federal government uses money for leverage, much as it did when it tied transportation funds to setting a fifty-five mile-per-hour speed limit. Federal funding represents about 7–8 percent of total public school revenues—not determinative but hardly trivial. Any state that chooses to opt out of NCLB—and none have yet done so—stands to lose a significant amount of scarce money. It is not an easy bargain, however. By taking federal money, states commit themselves to implementing a massive and detailed testing and sanctions regime, resulting in annual assessments of most students. The results of these tests will have significant consequences for any school or district that does not meet the state's standards of proficiency. As is the case with the tests themselves, states design many of the details about how these tests are used but must have their plans approved by the federal government.

No Child Left Behind is a reauthorization of the Elementary and Secondary Education Act of 1965, itself only one part of President Lyndon Johnson's War on Poverty. That measure distributed federal funds to local school districts on the basis of how many low-income students they served. While states can (and under NCLB must) sanc-tion poorly performing schools and districts in a variety of ways, the withholding of Title I funds is the only direct consequence that the federal government can apply to education at the state and local levels under No Child Left Behind. While all public (and many private) schools in a state will participate in NCLB's testing regimen, not every state has chosen to apply sanctions to non–Title I schools.[13]

The heart of the testing and sanctions regime under NCLB is something called adequate yearly progress (AYP). Making AYP is the defining quest for every school and district under No Child Left Behind. If they make AYP one year, school officials can start worrying about not making it the next year. If a school fails to make AYP, especially for two or more years in a row, the consequences become increasingly severe. AYP is based on the results of students' scores on standardized tests administered once a year. Achieving AYP means either that a sufficiently high percentage of the students in a school or district meets the state's standards for academic proficiency or that the school or district is demonstrating "continuous and substantial academic improvement for all students."[14] If a sufficiently high percentage of students does not meet that year's proficiency targets, a school or district can still make AYP if the number of students not achieving the standards has declined by 10 percent since the previous year—the "safe harbor" option.

Test results under NCLB are looked at in aggregate for all of the students in a grade level and for eight subgroups of students: for five racial and ethnic identifiers (white, black, Hispanic, American Indian, and Asian or Pacific Islander)[15] and for students who are eligible for free or reduced-priced lunches, those with limited English proficiency, and those who qualify for special education services. The idea of subgroup test proficiency is absolutely central to NCLB, both in its goals and in its implementation. Schools are judged by the performance of all of their students and by the performance of each of these eight subgroups. Critically, the proficiency test targets apply to a specific subgroup of students only if that school has enough students in that subgroup to trigger AYP evaluation. States vary considerably in their standards for what qualifies as the minimum number of students within a given group in a given grade level to trigger AYP evaluation for that subgroup, though the number generally ranges from ten to fifty.[16] The more qualifying subgroups that a school has, the more chances it has to fail, regardless of how it is doing in producing high-quality educational services or how successful it is with other subgroups of students. Large schools with diverse populations are, therefore, at a significant disadvantage.[17]

These proficiency requirements are combined with test participation requirements to ensure that school principals do not encourage some students to stay home on test day. The subgroup rule also applies to the separate evaluation of a school's participation rate: 95 percent of all eligible students within each grade and subgroup must show up to take the test.[18] There are also attendance requirements and graduation requirements that depend on the grade levels offered within a school. All of these requirements mean that there are currently thirty-six "possible ways for an individual school or district to fail to make AYP" for each grade level in a given school—eighteen for reading (nine for proficiency and nine for participation) and eighteen for math, assuming that the school has enough students to qualify for each subgroup at that grade level.[19] There are thirty-seven ways if one includes attendance or graduation standards for the entire school. It only takes failure in one subgroup in one subject in one grade to trigger AYP identification for that school or district.

These test results are cross-sectional, meaning that they take a snapshot of students (in aggregate or within a subgroup) at one point in the year. NCLB, therefore, bases its sanctions not on measuring what a school is adding to the achievement of individual students but on the aggregate peer performance of students as a whole or within a group. Schools are measured and weighed by their students, not their services. Proficiency targets are set by the state, approved by the federal Department of Education, and derived from baseline proficiency levels obtained from tests given during the 2001–2 school year. The bar gets higher every year until the 2013–14 school year, when 100 percent of a school's and district's students must meet these standards.

Since the law was first implemented, states have gradually added grade levels to the group of students tested. By the 2005–6 school year, all students in grades three through eight will have been tested in reading and mathematics and all high schools will test each subject once.[20] Science tests will be added by 2007–8, and President Bush has proposed expanding grade-level testing requirements in high schools. No Child Left Behind "applies the same high standards of academic achievement to all public elementary school and secondary school students," including students with disabilities and those with limited English proficiency.[21] Schools may make "reasonable adaptations and accommodations for students with disabilities";[22] however, the achievement of students with disabilities is still measured against the same state standards as the achievement of students without disabilities.[23] The law provides that any student who has attended school in the United States (except for Puerto Rico) for at least three consecutive years must be measured by the same proficiency tests, whether or not English is the student's native language. Schools are free to include, on a case-by-case basis, students who have been in the United States for less than three years. Students who have not been in U.S. schools for three consecutive years may be assessed using native-language instruments for two more consecutive years, provided that the "student has not yet reached a level of English language proficiency sufficient to yield valid and reliable information on what such student knows and can do on tests."[24]

Every year, each state educational agency must produce and distribute school report cards, which are required to provide concise and understandable information about student performance in each school (disaggregated by each of the eight subgroups that apply), graduation rates (if applicable), and the "professional qualifications" of the teachers disaggregated by the top and bottom quartiles of poverty in the state.[25] Parents of students in non-AYP schools can use these report cards to help them choose more successful schools when exercising their rights under the law.

For schools that fail to achieve their state's proficiency and participation targets, as a whole or for any one group with enough students (within a given group at grade level) to hit the subgroup trigger, or that fail to meet attendance or graduation requirements, the consequences become progressively more severe (table 1). While no sanctions are associated with the first year of AYP failure (other than the public identification of that school's status, usually in the local newspapers), being identified as a school that failed is a label that sticks, thereby setting the stage for the much more consequential sanctions that follow.

If a school fails to make AYP for a second consecutive year in the same subject area and grade level, it is identified as a "school in need of improvement." Those schools so identified that also receive Title I money must spend at least 10 percent of that money on professional development for teachers and principals but only on services that will improve academic achievement and remedy the deficiency that triggered the "in need of improvement" status. These schools must also notify their students' parents of this failure and allow them to transfer their children to public and charter schools within the district that are making the grade, giving "priority to the lowest achieving children from low-income families."[26] Districts cannot use lack of

TABLE 1.   Increasingly Severe Consequences for Schools That Fail to Make Adequate Yearly Progress

Consecutive Years of AYP failure (1)	Consequences for Individual Schools That Receive Monies for Disadvantaged Children under Title 1 (2)
2 years	Identified as "in need of improvement"
	School officials must . . .
	Develop a school improvement plan
	Spend at least 10% of Title I funds on professional development
	Allow parents to transfer their children to successful schools in the district
	Notify parents of their options under this plan
3 years	All consequences from previous years[a]
	School officials must . . .
	Implement school improvement plan
	Provide supplemental educational services for students
4 years	Corrective action
	This may include replacing staff, overhauling the curriculum, reducing management authority at the school level, hiring outside experts, or lengthening the school day and/or year.
5 years	Plan for restructuring
	Either by reconstituting school as a charter school, replacing all or most of the school personnel, contracting out for private management, state intervention, or other restructuring efforts
6 years	Initiate restructuring

[a]Each subsequent year continues consequences from all previous years

space or programs as an excuse, and they must spend 20 percent of their Title I money on transportation and other related services.[27] Districts must notify in writing all parents of students in the failing schools what being identified as a failing school means, what the school is trying to do in response, and what transfer options exist under the law.[28]

Schools that fail to make AYP for a third consecutive year must continue to provide parental choice and dedicate part of their Title I funds to professional development. These schools must also, however, begin to offer supplemental tutoring, remedial, and other academic services to their students, with providers chosen from a list of those approved by the state. These approved providers may include "faith-based" nonprofit entities as well as for-profit private-sector providers.[29] Again, these services are funded with a school's Title I money. A district receives no additional funds to comply with these requirements.

After a fourth year of failure, schools must take "corrective action" to meet the state's proficiency and participation goals for all applicable groups of students.[30] These schools must replace the school personnel "who are relevant to the failure to make adequate yearly progress," overhaul the school's curriculum, "decrease management authority at the school level," appoint "an outside expert to advise the school on its progress toward making adequate yearly progress," lengthen the school day or year, or restructure the "internal organizational structure of the school."[31]

If corrective action fails and the school finds itself on the failure list the next year, then the school must produce a plan for restructuring to be implemented in the next consecutive year of AYP failure. Restructuring is no small thing. It involves five basic options: reconstituting the failing school as a charter school, replacing "all or most of the school staff (which may include the principal) who are relevant to the failure to make adequate yearly progress," signing "a contract with an entity, such as a private management company," turning the operation of the school over to the state government, or any "other major restructuring of the school's governance arrangement that makes fundamental reforms."[32] Schools that have failed to make AYP in one or more years but make AYP the next year do not move up the consequence ladder. However, they are only taken off the list of failing schools if they make AYP for two consecutive years. After entering the school improvement phase and making AYP for one year, a school that fails to make AYP the next year moves on to the next level of consequences.

The law includes many other provisions, including requirements for ensuring that all academic teachers are "highly qualified," that all schools are safe and drug-free, consequences for entire school districts that fail to make AYP (based on the cumulative scores of all students in the district, a proviso that significantly improves the odds of targeting), along with technology-, reading-, and language-instruction initiatives. The law contains language to protect teachers, principals, and other educational professionals from "frivolous litigation" when trying to comply with the state's safe schools policies.

Although I focus on No Child Left Behind's effects on individual schools, entire school districts can also fail to make AYP based on the aggregate grade-level scores of all students in the district (also broken down by the eight subgroups). The most significant district-level consequence is the requirement to implement corrective action at the end of the fourth consecutive year of district AYP failure: districts can choose to defer program funds, implement curricular reforms, arrange for student transfer to another school district, overhaul the administration, or abolish the school district entirely.

How Is It Working?

Among the disagreements and controversies that surround the No Child Left Behind Act of 2001, researchers and policymakers agree on two things. First, the act's goals are laudable, even necessary. Ensuring that our public schools demonstrate improved performance for all students and for those students who have traditionally underperformed—including students of minority ethnicity, those from low-income households, and those with disabilities or limited English proficiency—is absolutely essential on the grounds of fairness, national economic interest, and fulfillment of the American dream.[33] Second, the law's effects are likely to be far-reaching. The sanctions to be imposed on schools that fail to make AYP clearly are significant, since they include restructuring and reconstituting failing public schools, perhaps under private management.

Beyond these points of agreement, however, very little is known about how the law will play out, not only because we remain in the early stages of implementing NCLB but also because the problem is both undertheorized and lacking in enough solid, nonpartisan, empirical research. Though recent work has examined the politics surrounding the law's passage and how and why it came to be,[34] much less work, at least by political scientists, has focused on the political and policy consequences of the law's implementation.

The little empirical evidence that exists on the achievement effects of No Child Left Behind is mixed. A March 2005 national survey of state and district education officials found that 72 percent of school districts reported that academic achievement was improving on the state-designed tests.[35] School district personnel uniformly reported that they were "aligning curriculum and instruction with standards and assessment (99%), and providing extra or more intensive instruction to low-achieving students (99%)."[36] The authors of an analysis of 320,000 student test scores from twenty-three states also found some evidence of improvement of mathematics and reading scores between the 2001–2 and 2003–4 school years. However, they observed that recent year-by-year growth in student test scores had declined since NCLB was put into place.[37] More alarmingly, the authors found that although growth in achievement levels has been declining for all ethnic groups, Hispanic students appeared to be falling behind white non-Hispanic students.[38]

In contrast to the relative lack of findings on the achievement effects of No Child Left Behind, an already large and still growing literature documents what is wrong with the law and what incremental fixes might be applied to it. Attacks on and critiques of No Child Left Behind are proliferating and are coming from many different sources focusing on many different consequences, intended and unintended. These worries center on a variety of issues that can be grouped into seven categories: the use of standardized tests; the use of cross-sectional test score data; the requirement for 100 percent proficiency; implementation, incentives, and uneven playing fields; unfunded mandates; lack of flexibility in implementation; and secondary provisions.

The use of standardized tests.   One group of critics focuses on the challenges of measuring anything as complex as student achievement with any set of standardized tests—no matter how thoroughly or thoughtfully implemented—and the consequences of these tests on the curricula and learning environments of schools. The danger is that in their single-minded desire to improve test scores, schools and teachers will damage the breadth and quality of the curriculum. This issue has been a topic of discussion ever since these tests were first implemented, as Superintendent Crawford noted.[39] Decisions about what to include on these tests are themselves highly political[40] and often result in a watered-down consensus curriculum that fails to make any real cognitive or evaluative demands on the students.

Deborah Meier, a former teacher and principal in Boston and New York and one of the strongest critics of No Child Left Behind, calls the current push for high-stakes standardized testing "fundamentally misguided," primarily because of the damage it will cause education as students experience it.[41] Rather than encourage the same kinds of qualities of leadership and governance that we would like to see in our students—the support and encouragement of local decision-making and citizen involvement—NCLB takes all power away from those closest to the creation of education and places it in the hands of distant "experts." As Meier observes, the use of standardized tests to improve education is based on a list of assumptions, none of which has been established beyond doubt:

There is a definition of what we mean by a good education.
Experts can know what this definition is.
Experts can measure it.
We can trust the experts more than we can trust the teachers and principals.
The system will produce equity in education, without major resource shifts.
The system will work.[42]

To which I would add:

We will know whether all this is working.

The use of cross-sectional test score data. Even if one believes that standardized tests can accurately and benignly measure student achievement, extracting what the school is doing for that student's achievement is much trickier than simply asserting how well one group of students is doing. No Child Left Behind currently relies on what is often called a "status model" of educational achievement that bases its assessments on a one-time snapshot of all of the students in a grade and in the grade-level subgroups.[43]

Using status models to measure the quality of education within a school has three main drawbacks. The first is the likelihood that schools will be designated as failing even though they are making gains: schools starting from extremely low levels of average proficiency cannot possibly expect to hit the targets before identification and sanction kick in. Theoretically, the "safe harbor" provision should protect such schools, but they must still reduce the number of students failing by 10 percent every year. If only one subgroup realizes smaller gains than other groups or schools as a whole, a school can still fail.[44]

A further complication is the issue of where to set the cutoff for triggering the inclusion of scores from specific subgroups in assessing whether a school is making AYP. Setting the trigger low (for example, ten students minimum per grade in any of the eight subgroups) increases the number of schools that qualify and, therefore, fail. Setting the trigger higher (fifty students in any given subgroup) runs the risk of ignoring the needs of minority students, since their results may not be directly looked at in schools with too few minority or high-need students to trigger the AYP evaluation for that subgroup. If the needs of specific subgroups of students are ignored, the basic premise of No Child Left Behind is lost.

The most important risk, however, is that basing sanctions on a status model also runs the considerable risk of identifying and sanctioning schools based mostly on the characteristics of the students rather than on the school's contribution to students' academic achievement, since many things outside of a school's control show up in the cross-sectional aggregation of student test scores.[45] I will take up this issue in considerable detail later in this volume. For now, however, it is useful to note that determining a school's success or failure based on these kinds of cross-sectional tests appears to result in incorrectly singling out schools with high-need populations.[46]

One hundred percent proficiency.   Closely related are potential problems resulting from the law's insistence on full proficiency as of 2013–14, when 100 percent of each school's and each district's students must be proficient in reading and mathematics. Critics have argued that this goal at best is overly ambitious and at worst is completely unattainable, leading to the prospect of failure for nearly all of the nation's public schools: "In 2003, no state or large district had anything close to 100% of their students performing at the *basic* level, much less the *proficient* level."[47] To attain 100 percent proficiency by 2013–14 would require a rate of improvement many times that which has been observed in recent years in even the most promising schools.[48]

The prospect of inevitable and widespread failure has led some observers and researchers to assert that the real goal of No Child Left Behind is the destruction of the public schools.[49] The challenge of 100 percent proficiency is especially problematic when one considers the prospect of full proficiency for special education students. Researchers have also pointed out that many special education students are so labeled because their disabilities prevent them from attaining grade-level proficiency, producing an inherent contradiction between definitions and goals.

Implementation, incentives, and uneven playing fields.   All policies have the potential for unforeseen and unwanted consequences, and No Child Left Behind is no different.[50] Critics have focused mostly on the skewed incentive structures that state, district, and school officials will face—that is, states face powerful incentives to set the proficiency bar as low as possible, given the costs involved in instituting the sanctions regime.[51] Teachers have incentives to cheat, while their leaders have incentives to look the other way if they feel that they will not be caught.[52] Districts have few incentives to accept poor and minority students from other districts (unless they are forced to do so), and schools might be encouraged to move their lower-performing students out of regular education and into alternative learning centers or high school equivalency programs.[53] Given the malleability of and tremendous variance in how states define academic proficiency, many potential problems arise with the utility and reliability of data. A report by the U.S. General Accounting Office cautioned that "more than half of the state and school district officials . . . interviewed reported by being hampered by poor and unreliable student data."[54]

Although the federal Department of Education must approve states' plans, the standards and assessments that states use are typically based on preexisting accountability systems, which may or may not have overlapped with NCLB's goals and methods, creating a very messy patchwork of tests. This tremendous state variation in baseline levels of proficiency means that a successful school in one state could easily be classified as failing in another state that set its initial proficiency targets at a higher level.[55] The General Accounting Office also found a great deal of variance in how and how well states were measuring academic proficiency in these early stages of implementation, leading, for example, California to require that only 14 percent of its elementary students be proficient and Colorado to require 78 percent proficiency in the same year.[56] According to Minnesota's Office of the Legislative Auditor, "Due to inter-state differences in proficiency standards, testing practices, and 'adequate yearly progress' calculations, there is no meaningful way to use AYP data to make multi-state comparisons of educational performance."[57]

Other implementation worries focus not on the failure of the law, its goals, or its methods but on the school, district, and state officials who are supposed to be carrying out NCLB's reforms. Of particular concern are levels of compliance and the pace of implementation of parental exit options in failing schools (which apply to schools that have failed to make AYP for two consecutive years). Very small percentages of parents who are eligible to send their children to successful schools appear to be doing so, and only a slightly larger percentage of parents whose children are eligible for supplemental services take advantage of that option. Lack of capacity in successful schools, lack of information on the part of parents, and active district resistance may have combined to prevent large numbers of parents from exercising their exit options.[58]

Unfunded mandates.   Claims that No Child Left Behind does not adequately fund the ambitious goals and requirements that it places on states and districts have come from all levels of the public educational system. At the district level, such costs include the requirement to comply with the fully trained teacher requirement, the provision of supplemental services, and the task of administering and grading the ever-increasing volume of tests. At the state level, these costs include implementing all of the corrective action and restructuring provisions as well as overseeing the testing regimen.[59] Ted Kennedy, who helped steer the bill through the Senate, later lamented, "The tragedy is that these long overdue reforms are finally in place, but the funds are not."[60]

In April 2005, school districts in several states joined the National Education Association in suing Secretary of Education Margaret Spellings on the basis of insufficient funding of NCLB.[61] Though the law states, "Nothing in this Act shall be construed to . . . mandate a State or any subdivision thereof to spend any funds or incur any costs not paid for under this Act,"[62] the plaintiffs argued that the compliance requirements placed an unfunded and undue financial burden on local schools and districts. The U.S. General Accounting Office concluded that No Child Left Behind was not an unfunded mandate because participation in NCLB is technically voluntary and the conditions laid out in the law "were a condition of federal financial assistance," thus disqualifying NCLB as an unfunded mandate as defined by law.[63] A February 2005 report by the National Council of State Legislatures, argued that No Child Left Behind's ambiguous and coercive provisions fail to pass constitutional muster.[64] In addition, observers have expressed concern that rigidities in the provisions for schools that fail to make AYP will make academic improvement less rather than more likely as insufficient monies are spread too thinly and are used only in crisis mode.

Lack of flexibility in implementation.   Reports from the field also indicate a great deal of frustration on the part of school, district, and state officials regarding their lack of flexibility in complying with the law's underlying goals. Of particular concern are rigid and unrealistic targets of academic success, particularly for students receiving special education services and those with limited English proficiency. In its 2005 task force report, the National Conference of State Legislatures concluded that "states should be allowed to develop any system they choose as long as it meets the spirit of NCLB."[65] The report also argued that a preexisting statutory basis for this much-needed flexibility lies in provisions allowing the U.S. Department of Education to offer statutory waivers to states, districts, and schools.[66]

Secondary provisions.   Small but significant provisions continue to come to light, such as the withholding of all federal funds for school districts that fail to notify their state's educational administration that "no policy of the local educational agency prevents, or otherwise denies participation in, constitutionally protected prayer in public elementary schools and secondary schools."[67] Funds are also to be withheld from districts that "deny equal access [to] any group affiliated with the Boy Scouts of America" or any other group listed as a "patriotic society" as well as from districts that fail to "provide, on a request made by military recruiters or an institution of higher education access to secondary school students' names, addresses, and telephone listings."[68]

In response to these concerns, researchers and policymakers have proposed a series of modifications to No Child Left Behind.

1. Fully funding the law

No Child Left Behind's passage was accompanied by promises of significant increases in funding. Officials in several states are now complaining that the additional monies allocated by the federal government do not even cover the costs of compliance, much less those necessary to achieve meaningful progress in closing the achievement gap.[69] The combined concerns of unfunded mandates and the increased federal intrusion into state policy-making have sparked legal and political opposition among a very diverse group of stakeholders that runs the gamut from teachers' unions to Republican governors and legislators.

On April 20, 2005, the Utah legislature voted to instruct state school leaders to focus on Utah's goals and priorities and to ignore provisions of NCLB that conflicted with the state's plan; Utah's governor signed the measure the following month. The bill did not directly withdraw Utah from NCLB but increased the likelihood of a showdown over the state's autonomy and put $76 million in federal education funding at risk.[70] Republican U.S. Representative Steve Mascaro was quite blunt: "I'd just as soon they take the stinking money and go back to Washington with it. Let us resolve our education problems by ourselves. I will not be threatened by Washington over $76 million."[71] The following August, Connecticut sued the federal government to reclaim $50 million in state money spent on compliance. Though the amount was small, observers cited the symbolic importance of the suit, arguing that the "real battle is over who will make key education decisions—local officials or policymakers in Washington."[72] These political rifts are likely only to deepen as NCLB's sanctions sweep up more and more schools, thereby forcing states to cope with the attendant costs.

2. Moving away from status models of measurement

Many reform proposals focus on the way in which achievement is measured. One proposed change is to look at the year-by-year changes in percentages of students who achieve academic proficiency rather than the percentages of students who are or are not meeting the targets. This approach is usually referred to as a "growth model."[73] A second approach is to use what is called a "value-added" model of achievement, which attempts to extract the value a school adds to a given student's achievement by tracking the changes in test scores over time for individual students.[74] I will discuss both of these modifications in some detail later in this volume. Neither is perfect, and each raises its own challenges, but either might be preferable to the status model currently embodied in the law.

3. Providing more flexibility and more realism

Some observers have argued that the requirement for 100 percent proficiency should be amended or scaled back to account for the almost impossible nature of its attainment: "there should be evidence that the goal does not exceed that [which] has previously been achieved by the highest performing schools."[75] Others have argued for a more realistic and flexible approach to the testing of and achievement standards for students with limited English proficiency and those with disabilities.[76] Critics have also declared that the 10 percent growth requirement necessary to achieve safe harbor cannot be attained by all but a very small number of schools not making AYP.[77]

4. Increasing coherence and consistency between states, particularly in the definition of academic proficiency

More standardization of accountability systems would not only be fairer but also provide researchers with much more reliable data on which to base any evaluations of NCLB's effects on achievement.[78]

What Is Still Missing from the Debate

Of all the problems with No Child Left Behind, the ultimate success or failure of its ambitious agenda will likely come down to how the law interacts with two unavoidable realities in American education.

The first reality is that the United States has a very unequal and class-stratified society.[79] Most children go to school with children from families with similar incomes. However ambitious, No Child Left Behind does nothing to address these long-standing resource inequalities in the United States and its educational system. To the extent that these resource inequalities—rather than failures by administrators, principals, and/or teachers—are responsible for unequal academic achievement, No Child Left Behind is destined to fail to live up to its liberal promises.

The second reality is that education involves a great deal of uncertainty on the part of those who would evaluate it and a great deal of discretion on the part of those who perform its tasks.[80] In other words, it is very hard to know what is actually happening at the moment of "education." In all of the debate about No Child Left Behind, policymakers have failed to ask the most basic and most important question: Can we ever really know if a child's education is good?

So many factors contribute to and confound what ultimately happens at the interface between a student's mind and the school's products that policymakers should think very carefully about how to measure "educational quality." Doing so will require a deeper and more thorough investigation of the underlying problem of producing and measuring quality in education. It may seem like an obscure task, but, as I hope will become apparent, it represents the first step on an interesting and necessary journey to achieve a vision of equality of educational outcomes for all students, especially for those students whose dreams have been continually deferred.

This book argues primarily that policymakers must begin with the goal of producing quality in education and move from there rather than assume that any test can accurately measure "good" education. This approach is radical in the literal sense of getting to the roots of the challenge at hand. We cannot succeed without doing so. If—and this is a big if—we accept the limitations of our evaluative capabilities, and if we get beyond the magical thinking of NCLB's punishment-driven philosophy, then we can make the law live up to its liberal promises.

Chapter 2, "The Problem of Quality," lays out the foundational arguments of the book with an exploration of two questions:

What determines educational quality?

How, if at all, can we observe and identify it?

To answer these questions, I explore the ephemeral nature of assessing quality in education. I take a detour into what economists and scholars of organizations can tell us about designing systems of measurements and rewards to lay the groundwork for a more effective way of going about things under No Child Left Behind.

Chapter 3, "Making the Grade (or Not): Success and Failure in NCLB's World," begins the book's empirical analyses by taking a broad look at how schools fare under the law and how success and failure in No Child Left Behind's peculiar world are determined by phenomena over which schools have absolutely no control. I combine a discussion of national developments with original data from a survey of Minnesota school principals as a way to explore the complex reality of school success and failure:

> Why do schools succeed or fail to make adequate yearly progress?
>
> Given the dominance of race, ethnicity, and inequality in determining achievement test scores, do school principals' actions matter at all in measuring educational achievement?

Chapter 4, "Top-Down and Bottom-Up: NCLB, Charter Schools, and the Public School Principalship," examines two sets of questions about the connection between NCLB and the behaviors and attitudes of the principals who are ultimately responsible for what happens inside the school. The first set of questions concerns the effects of No Child Left Behind on what principals do, how they spend their time, and what they think about their influence:

> What do public school principals think about No Child Left Behind?
>
> What effects does the law have on leadership within the public schools?

The second set of questions concerns the critical but mostly overlooked issue of how No Child Left Behind interacts with the other major reform effort already under way in the United States, which is the introduction of competition to public schooling, whether in the form of charter schools, public school choice, or vouchers for private schools. I focus on the connection between the provision of parental choices in education and NCLB's top-down accountability approach, asking:

> How does doing top-down accountability and bottom-up school choice at the same time affect the quality of the public school principalship ? Do the two approaches reinforce each other, or do they get in each other's way?
> Is sanction better than competition?

Charter schools are in a unique position as both targets and solutions under No Child Left Behind. They are subject to the same tests and sanctions as their traditional public school counterparts; however, they also constitute one of the options for reconstituting a failing school in the later stages of NCLB implementation. In spite of charters' involvement with both top-down and bottom-up reforms, their placement as such has not received enough attention in the literature.

Chapter 5, "Rethinking Assessment," takes up only one question, but it is an important one:

> If we wish to preserve the goals and achieve the purported benefits of NCLB, can we do a better job?

I examine two commonly discussed alternatives to the cross-sectional testing: comparing schools on the year-by-year changes in percentages of students making proficiency targets and comparing schools based on changes in individual student test scores over time. I also suggest a new alternative: using, in a meaningful way, the opinions of those closest to the production of the good and the bad in education in our assessments of schools.

In chapter 6, "Carrots, Sticks, and Unbroken Windows: Making NCLB Live Up to Its Promises," I propose that we take these lessons about measuring educational quality as a basis for trying to make No Child Left Behind fulfill its goals. I offer a series of increasingly substantial modifications to or revisions of No Child Left Behind that will get us closer to realizing the critical vision of academic equality embodied in the law. We should directly measure leadership and quality within the institutions rather than just trying to extract this information from student test scores. We should also include meaningful rewards in the incentive structure that we create based on these assessments.

No Child Left Behind has received considerable attention, an unsurprising development given both the ambitious goals embodied in the law and the significant effects that its implementation has had and will continue to have. Because we remain in the early stages of the law's implementation, relatively little peer-reviewed scholarly work has been published on the topic.[81] This book seeks in part to help remedy this deficiency.

This book's value ultimately will be determined by practitioners and stakeholders in all levels of U.S. education, from parents to policymakers. I hope that the book will be relevant beyond its immediate subject. Many states, including those with Republican governors and legislatures, are growing increasingly uncomfortable with the federal government's reach into what has traditionally been the purview of state and local governments. NCLB will come up for reauthorization in 2007. It could be gutted, revoked, or starved, the preferred way of killing a policy that benefits populations that are seen as deserving. Regardless of what happens with No Child Left Behind, however, high-stakes accountability will remain a central part of the education reform debate for the foreseeable future.

Three conditions are likely to endure in U.S. educational policy: a desire to improve academic achievement among traditionally underperforming students, the struggle with the problem of how to do so, and the related challenge of assessing whether what we are doing works. This book seeks primarily to help create a framework that will allow us to respond to these challenges in closing the achievement gap.

Perhaps a course for policymakers—something along the lines of Measuring and Producing Educational Quality 101—would be useful. If I were to offer such a course, I would begin with the lessons learned and the lessons not learned since Superintendent King's unfortunate experiment. I would take my students down the long and winding road of understanding the importance of resource inequalities in education; the challenge of measuring what is good and what is not good; and the importance of leadership, organization, and incentives. In attempting to find and support this ephemeral thing called a good education, I would end with the hopeful caution that we not leave our common sense behind while we try to move these mountains.

CHAPTER 2

The Problem of Quality

How do you improve your educational product
when you can neither describe the product nor
explain how it is produced?

James Q. Wilson, Bureaucracy

What, exactly, do teachers and principals do with and for children
when they are at school? Parents send their children to school for the
better part of their waking lives but rarely have much of an idea about
what has happened at the critical interface between their minds and
the variety of experiences they encounter and in which they have
engaged. At the end of the school day, parents will ask their child,
"So, how was school today?" and she will probably say, "Fine."[1]

The problem is that no one else really knows, either, at least not
with absolute certainty. The child's teacher—if he is attentive and
responsive—probably has a better idea about how well the student is
doing than anyone else, especially if the child is young. But even the
child's teacher cannot tell for sure whether the student is engaging
with the material or whether her peers and parents are reinforcing or
undermining his efforts. Chances are that the principal does not
know more than the teacher. She probably has a pretty good assessment of her teachers' level of effort and competence, but when she
walks through the door, she witnesses a performance rather than an

accurate picture of what goes on day to day—although the principal of course knows this.

The principal's administrative superiors know even less than the principal does, but because they are living under No Child Left Behind, they assign standardized tests to the students. These tests may measure some things more or less accurately but have their own consequences. The teacher—if he feels that there will be real effects from his students' test scores—may alter his teaching to have the students perform better on the tests. If we did not like what the teacher was doing, such changes may be beneficial. The problem, of course, is that we did not know what he was doing in the absence of our test, so we cannot ever say if his reorientation was good or bad.

It is hardly a trivial problem. Any accountability program such as No Child Left Behind must accurately measure what a given school or teacher is adding to the knowledge and skills of a given student, above and beyond the following:

how innately "smart" the student is;
how well prepared the student was before coming to this
    school or to this teacher;
how rich or poor the student is;
how well the student has mastered standard English;
how chaotic or predictable the student's life is;
how healthy the student is;
how hungry the student is;
how motivated the student is;
how much the student's peers reinforce or hinder the school
    or teacher's efforts;
how involved the parents are;
how helpful their involvement is;
how safe the school is; and
how clean, toxin-free, and well-equipped the school is.

Filtering out all of these factors is not an easy task, even when the body politic is united in the underlying goal of what constitutes a "good" education, which may or may not be the case today. But this is exactly what No Child Left Behind purports to do.

In this chapter I begin with the most basic and most challenging questions when thinking about NCLB's prospects:

What determines educational quality?

How, if at all, can we observe and identify it?

Answering these questions requires a bit of thinking about how, if at all, any public policy can secure excellence amid so much uncertainty and complexity. Though I will digress into a bit of economics and organizational theory, understanding how organizations cope with complexity is critical to evaluating No Child Left Behind's effects on the public schools. Both NCLB's proponents and its opponents have gotten a bit ahead of themselves in trying to envision the long-term effects of this law without adequately considering the basic challenge that we may never be able to measure with perfect certainty how well a school or a teacher is doing with any single measure of educational performance. In this book, I also ask readers to adopt the point of view of a public school principal trying to achieve academic excellence in her school while confronting many demands on her time, many limitations on her power, and ambitious and hasty reform efforts—like No Child Left Behind.

Researchers have tended to focus exclusively on broader issues such as the politics of implementation and the patterns of district-level changes in test scores, without sufficiently examining the messy details of how this law affects the production of education and the behaviors of those supervising this process in the schools. Therefore, good reasons exist for my focus on school principals, even though parents, teachers, and students constitute other important factors in the enterprise. First and foremost, No Child Left Behind targets schools, not classrooms or individual students. School principals ultimately bear responsibility for and are held accountable for the results of NCLB's tests and sanctions: "As with so many other educational mandates and regulations, no matter what their origin, many of these related to NCLB eventually fall to the principal to carry out. . . .

[P]rincipals already accustomed to being the instructional leaders of their schools will now have a whole new set of federally mandated responsibilities and requirements telling them just what 'instructional leadership' means."[2]

Second, leadership matters. How much leadership, under what conditions, and how to improve it are all very complex and highly debated issues. In spite of my focus on principals, I hope that parents, teachers, and students will benefit from this book and that it will resonate with their experiences. School principals are critical to educational quality; however, they can do only so much, bound as they are by a web of competing demands and situations to which they must constantly react and acting as they do within a policy framework that they can only shape at the margins. If I ask readers to adopt the point of view of the school principal, I also ask them to accept that principals do what they do in an environment characterized by complexity, uncertainty, and difficult trade-offs. Education is very, very complicated, as is the measurement of its quality.

Things That Schools Can and Cannot Control

When considering educational quality, educational policy experts have debated what to emphasize. Should we focus on all of those things that principals and teachers do within the school? Should we focus on all of those things over which schools have little or no control but that students bring with them, such as ability, previous schooling, parental involvement, poverty, languages, motivations, and many other factors?

Each side has had its proponents. Those who would focus on those aspects of the production of educational quality over which schools have no control often cite the 1966 *Report on Equality of Educational Opportunity* as at least one of the foundations for their views. Employing surveys of nearly 650,000 students in the United States, James Coleman and his colleagues sought primarily to highlight the persistent patterns of and damaging consequences arising from racial segregation in American schools.

The report concluded that racial segregation was so damaging because community characteristics dominated school characteristics in the production of academic achievement, a finding that continues to influence educational policy today: "When [socioeconomic factors] are statistically controlled, however, it appears that differences in schools account for only a small fraction of differences in pupil achievement."[3] By focusing on the importance of factors that schools cannot control, Coleman and his coauthors provided considerable ammunition to those who would argue against any kind of systematic plan for improving school performance.

In this view, educational quality depends mostly on the students' lives outside of the school environment, including the challenges raised by growing up in resource-poor communities. Under NCLB, all of the factors that affect measured achievement but lie beyond a school's control will largely determine that school's success or failure. Some researchers have pointed out the incongruity of failing to address long-standing resource inequalities in any educational reform effort.[4] By omitting any attempt to fix or even acknowledge that resources and communities matter for academic achievement, No Child Left Behind assumes that "schools by themselves can achieve dramatic, totally unprecedented, levels of academic achievement for all racial and ethnic groups as well as for children with disabilities, low-income children, and children without English fluency—all in a short space of time."[5]

Perhaps the quality problem in education is really a poverty problem. However, framing the problems of the achievement gap in these terms offers little help in determining what to do with No Child Left Behind now that we have it. I will, therefore, focus on those factors that schools can control. Coleman and his colleagues also found that differences between the quality of schools mattered more for disadvantaged than advantaged children, belying the more pessimistic interpretations of their report's findings. These forty-year-old conclusions lend support to the foundation of No Child Left Behind's liberal agenda. If we can get accountability right, then the poorest and most disenfranchised students might benefit the most.

Unfortunately, the challenges that context brings to academic achievement are even deeper and more complicated than resource inequalities and segregation. Coleman and his coauthors also found that the quality of a student's peer group factored heavily into her achievement. Peers matter. Being around motivated, smart, and well-educated students makes a child learn more, regardless of what the school is doing.

Economists put education into the category of public goods—that is, things whose benefits flow to everyone whether or not they contribute. Other public goods include clean air, a nice fireworks display, and a strong national defense. Though everyone may wish to have these things, their provision is not likely to be as vigorous or plentiful as some people may want because some individuals will choose to enjoy the benefits without contributing to the cost. Economists dub this phenomenon free riding.[6] A related problem, more relevant to education, is the problem of "congestion effects"—difficulties that arise when the inability to exclude people from receiving the benefits of a public good results in too many people using the service. Urban freeways, for example, can become so congested that drivers end up going more slowly than they would like. Many of these users would willingly pay more to reduce congestion but are not always allowed to do so.

In education, congestion effects are most notable in the fact that the misbehavior of one student negatively affects the amount of teacher attention and the quality of services received by all of the other students.[7] Researchers have confirmed empirically what teachers know intuitively: peers matter to the academic achievement of the other students in the classroom and school.[8] A small number of researchers—economists mostly—have explored the problems of congestion effects in education, using mathematical modeling techniques to show that peer effects explain much of the typical educational structure, including

- why private schools offer scholarships to poorer kids who are good students (because the benefit of the student to the quality of education received by all of the other, paying students is worth more to the private school than the scholarship);[9]
- why we allow college classes of two hundred or more students but would never tolerate that in kindergarten (because the disruptive behaviors and costs associated with

congestion effects are—we hope—much more prevalent
with five-year-olds than with nineteen-year-olds);[10]

- why researchers do not find that reducing class sizes
improves academic performance (because class sizes are
already optimized to account for potential congestion
effects).[11]

While private school principals and administrators can compensate for the challenges of peer effects through their ability to offer
scholarships for "good" students and threaten expulsion for "bad"
ones, public school leaders have far fewer tools for controlling the
composition of their peer groups. To the extent that peer effects
determine educational achievement, the public schools will always
underperform their private school counterparts, stuck as the public
schools are with whatever children come through the doors.

Public school managers can control many things, of course, and
educational policy research has a long tradition that says we should
focus on getting more of these kinds of leadership behaviors and
characteristics in our schools rather than waving our hands and saying that parents, peers, and communities determine everything in
children's academic achievement. Proponents of this "effective
schools" approach to educational reform have asserted that it makes
more sense to focus on the quality of production processes than to
use standardized achievement test results that capture mostly student's experiences outside of the production process.

Ronald Edmonds, an administrator in New York City's public
schools and a professor at Harvard University, is often credited as a
founder of the effective schools movement. Two things characterized
Edmonds's approach and shaped much of the research that would
follow. First, effective schools focused on the need to improve urban
education, foreshadowing what we now call the "achievement gap."
Rejecting the pessimistic interpretations of the Coleman report,
Edmonds critiqued the emphasis on family background as "absolving
educators of their professional responsibility to be instructionally
effective."[12] Second, in Edmonds's framework, leadership mattered.
Bringing together earlier disparate studies, Edmonds highlighted six
of the "most tangible and indispensable characteristics of effective

schools and their leaders." Effective schools were characterized by "strong administrative leadership, without which the disparate elements of good schooling can neither be brought together nor kept together."[13] These leaders fostered a climate of high expectations and orderly and humane learning climates and focused first and foremost on having students learn the basics, diverting resources from other efforts when necessary and constantly monitoring whether students were mastering these basic skills and concepts.[14]

The early efforts of Edmonds and others spurred an explosion of studies and reform efforts based on the philosophy of the effective school. These evaluations typically relied on case studies or on comparisons of student test scores and shared the basic approach of comparing effective to ineffective schools. In general, the findings and results of the follow-up studies mirrored those of the early researchers. Active leadership by school principals mattered. Safety, order, a focus on the basics, high expectations (by staff as well as teachers), and an active role in instruction all appeared to be associated with educational effectiveness.[15] Getting parents involved also mattered.

A subset of studies on effective schools focused specifically on the fact that schools are social systems, not factories, and complex interpersonal relationships can reinforce or subvert leaders' efforts. Fostering a social environment characterized by trust and feelings of empowerment among students, teachers, and school principals could improve instruction.[16] Although schools' social conditions factored into Edmonds's and others' research, thinking about school communities adds some nontrivial complications to the hope of successfully implementing—and especially replicating—effective schools programs.

Unfortunately, in spite of much effort, the effective schools movement did not achieve its promise of unequivocal and sustained achievement gains in America's largest urban communities. Subsequent researchers pointed to several problems with and limitations of the research.[17] First, researchers tended to focus on observing the leadership characteristics of a few high-achieving schools. Such case selection made it impossible to determine whether good leadership had caused or resulted from high achievement or whether some other unobserved factors accounted for both phenomena.

Serious measurement problems also arose. Not only is there much debate about how to measure academic achievement, but each of the contributors to an excellent academic environment is difficult to measure in its own right. In addition, changing administrative behavior necessitates difficult trade-offs, especially of time, a principal's scarcest resource. The effective schools literature offers little guidance on, for example, when a principal should take away time from supervising teachers in favor of reaching out to the parent community. Finally, all of the components of an effective school are interrelated, perhaps reinforcing each other in ways not fully understood. Some school characteristics, for example, may be of more use in poorer communities than wealthier communities, but simple lists will not get at these important secondary considerations. Absent any clear idea of which elements of the effective schools menu matter the most, policymakers can offer little guidance on how to get there from here. Although promising, the effective schools literature offers only a checklist, not a recipe.

So, do society or schools matter to educational quality? Of course, the answer is both. The question is whether policymakers can disentangle the effects of factors such as resource inequalities that schools cannot control and the polity chooses not to fix from those things that can be fixed within schools. This poses enough of a challenge; however, yet another issue must be considered. Even if researchers and policymakers can agree on a set of effective school characteristics, they cannot simply announce, "Let's have better discipline and more enthusiastic teachers!" and have it happen. Rather, two closely related problems arise. The first involves thinking about educational production. The second involves questions of agency.

Production, Agency, and Information

In economics, a production function tells you how different inputs translate into the maximum possible amount of your final product. For example, so much machinery combined with so many person-hours of work will allow a firm to produce some number of cars or refrigerators. The primary purpose of a production function is to tell the managers of a firm the level of maximum output that their firm can produce given the optimal combination of inputs. The process sounds very straightforward, but applying this logic to education is highly problematic.

What exactly, is the "maximum" output of a school? Certainly not the throughput—that is, the number of students moved through the system—especially if they have not learned very much. But trying to think about measuring the maximum amount of learning a school can produce raises serious measurement challenges. Consider, for example, the simplified model of educational production presented in figure 1.[18] This model shows three basic inputs that produce academic achievement in a given school: student quality, school quality, and peer quality. Of course, each of these inputs is complicated in its own right, but this model assumes that the right combination of student factors, school factors, and peer factors produces the maximum possible academic achievement for a given student.

One problem with the model in figure 1 is that it offers no insight into which of these components matters most to high-quality education. Economists usually add a Greek letter or arithmetic function to each of the elements of the production function to capture the fact that different inputs are best used in different amounts. For the purposes of illustration, we could also choose to represent visually the differential impact of the three components of the education production function. Consider, for example, modifying the function as by resizing the various components of academic achievement (figure 2). Here, student factors dominate academic achievement, and the school factors play into achievement only at the margins, a model consistent with the findings of the Coleman report and with decades of research into effective schools. In addition, the various components of the basic educational production function are often incorrectly aggregated. For example, the school factors variable in the simple model of figure 1 is supposed to refer only to a given student's experience of the school factors, not all of her peers' experiences.[19] In the real world, however, we measure these school factors only in aggregate and assume that the school experience is uniform for all students, which is never the case. School inputs, for example, may very well differ or have different effects in wealthier or poorer communities.

The biggest problem with the model in figures 1 and 2, however, is that each of the components on the right side of the model is itself

Academic achievement for the student	=	Student Quality	+	School Quality	+	Peer Quality

Fig. 1. **Production in education. (Based on Hanushek 1972, 1979; Summers and Wolfe 1977.)**

Academic achievement for the student	=	Student Quality	+	School Quality	+	Peer Quality

Fig. 2. **Production in education, modified**

the product of many factors, and some elements contribute to more than one component of our simple model. Consider the expanded educational production function in figure 3. Here, each of the four factors in the initial model is broken into separate equations, thereby showing just how complex the picture is. The measurement of achievement complicates what should be the most straightforward part of the picture—the test score of a given student. The achievement that a particular student demonstrates on a particular day, however, is determined not only by all of the factors on the right side of the equation but also by factors specific to the test and the day of the test, including how well the test is constructed, how focused the student is, and no small amount of statistical noise.

Even if we assume away all of these complications, the picture is anything but simple. Student quality depends on many interrelated factors, such as how hard the student works, how helpful her parents are, and what role her peers take. Peer quality is similarly intricate and contextual. Most important, for my purposes, the school-quality part of the equation depends to some extent on things that public school principals can control (leadership quality), some things that they can control only imperfectly (teacher quality and parental involvement), and many things that they cannot control at all (financial resources).

The various components in figure 3 are also as related to each other as they are to academic achievement. Parental involvement, for

Measured academic achievement	=	Student Quality	+	School Quality	+	Peer Quality
=		=		=		=
True academic achievement		Innate ability		School resources		Peer ability
+		+		+		+
Past academic achievement		*Parental involvement*		Leadership quality		*Peer effort*
+		+		+		
Test factors		*Student effort*		Teaching quality		
+				+		
Test-taking factors				*Parental involvement*		
+						
Noise						

Fig. 3. The components of educational production, an incomplete list. (Underlined items indicate phenomena that No Child Left Behind seeks directly to change. Items in italics indicate factors that NCLB attempts to change indirectly, through changes to the underlined items.)

example, likely affects both the things that students bring with them and school efforts to make the most of the students that they have. Each of these components is likely to be difficult to quantify and measure even if their independent effects could be teased out, and they do not work independently.[20] Strong leadership and strong teaching, for example, can encourage higher levels of parental involvement, individual student effort, and peer effort. The key point in figure 3, however, is that No Child Left Behind attempts to use an indirect measure of "true" achievement to extract the quality of leadership and teaching in a school in spite of the complexity of the task. Policymakers might be better served by trying to measure the quality of leadership and teaching as directly as possible rather than trying to extract it from the results of tests given to a group of students on a given day.

The fact that measurable elements of the education production function, such as smaller class sizes, have not been directly linked to sustained achievement gains has led to a considerable debate about whether inputs, especially money, matter at all in education.[21] In short, no research consensus indicates that spending more money on any specific input will lead to higher-quality education. No Child Left Behind has inherited the skeptical attitude of this debate with its exclusive focus on outputs and sanctions and its notable omission of any financial or bureaucratic rewards for successful schools. Thinking about NCLB or any other high-stakes testing policy in this way clearly demonstrates that this is a very indirect way of going about things. Moreover, No Child Left Behind uses only punishment or the threat of punishment to change the behaviors of teachers and administrators, and it takes on the aura of magical thinking. Wave the wand (the threat of sanction) based on these test scores and hope for the best.

Unfortunately, this story features yet another complication. Even if test scores accurately separate good and bad leadership and teaching, it may not be possible to make principals and teachers do what we want them to do or stop doing what we do not want them to do. This problem is one of agency.[22] Economists and political scientists have spent much time thinking about how institutions get people to behave in certain ways. Many of these models divide people who are involved in these kinds of relationships into two groups, principals and agents. In this perspective, principals do not refer to school principals but to actors trying to control other people's behavior. This other person is the agent.[23] Agency relationships are present in almost all aspects of our lives—when we try to get good produce at the grocery store, when we try to get the local factory not to degrade our drinking water, or when we try to get our elected politicians to represent our interests.

Political scientist Terry M. Moe has framed the challenges of No Child Left Behind specifically in terms of agency relationships.[24] The central challenge of agency is securing compliance in an environment characterized by incomplete and unevenly distributed information. Economists call these challenges informational asymmetries.[25] Our elected congressional representatives may know if they are wasting public money, but we may lack this knowledge. Our teachers may know if they are doing a good job, but we may not be able to tell. We could try to monitor their behavior, but watching over our agents all of the time is very expensive and time-consuming. We have no choice but to try to choose good agents, monitor them as best we can, and then trust them. Because we cannot measure how hard or well our agents are working, we run the risk that they will either slack off or that they will actively work against our goals. This is the problem of moral hazard. Lacking sufficient information about what our agents are doing, we run the risk that our agents will choose not to work or to work in ways that we do not want.[26]

The challenges of agency are more of a problem in education than in most other agency relationships because of the ephemeral nature of the service whose quality is being (or not being) observed. It is very difficult to observe the "true" quality of what a school principal or teacher is doing, which in turn makes controlling their behavior very difficult. The answer that economists offer is for an organization to try to devise a system of incentives that will align agents' decisions regarding how to do their jobs with the organization's goals.[27] The adequate provision of incentives, however, requires that someone, somewhere knows how to observe the true quality of an enterprise. In education, this is anything but certain.

A key question to address in the bureaucratic world of No Child Left Behind is how the law deals with agency and informational asymmetries. The answer is that NCLB does not deal with these asymmetries, at least not directly.[28] It does not restructure the agreements between administrators and principals (at least not until the year of reconstitution) or between principals and their teachers. NCLB's faith in the transformative power of punishment (or the threat of punishment) includes quite a bit of optimism and is at odds with what educators know about behavioral change.

There are, however, more thoughtful ways to consider the challenges. For political scientist James Q. Wilson, the primary way to understand an organization is to look at what it does, especially the degree to which two aspects of that organization's production can be measured. The first is the set of outputs, or what the people in the firms do when they are working. The second is the set of outcomes, or what the firms produce.[29] For Wilson, serious challenges arise when either outputs or outcomes are difficult to measure. When neither is measurable, then considerable problems of supervision and control arise. This is education at its core.

It is difficult to reward excellence and sanction mediocrity in education because it is difficult to obtain objective measures of performance. Therefore, leaders tend to focus on what they can measure, are often loath to let subordinates have too much discretion, and end up trying to maintain order more than achieve excellence. Wilson calls these troublesome enterprises "coping organizations," based on the fact that their managers spend a lot of time just coping. Schools are perhaps the archetypal examples of Wilson's conception of a coping organization.[30] Coping organizations are characterized by conflicts between managers and staff and between regulators and managers. They are also characterized by an intense desire to avoid risks and the consequent following to the letter of standard operating procedures: "In coping organizations . . . management will have a strong incentive to focus their efforts on the most easily measured (and thus most easily controlled) activities of their operators. They cannot evaluate or often even see outcomes, and so only the brave manager will be inclined to give much freedom to subordinates."[31] Wilson therefore believes that "effective management is almost impossible" in schools and other coping organizations.[32]

This apparent failure of management is actually the result of a rational decision process. If a school principal knows that no one will ever accurately gauge the results of her efforts, then there are few incentives to take the kinds of risks that might produce higher-quality education, though many principals and teachers do so anyway. All coping organizations, however, do not face equal informational challenges or have equal ability to respond to these challenges. Organizations that must respond to their customers' ability to leave will have a better idea of the quality of their product and therefore will do a better job. Those firms that rely on customer exit and entry rather than administrative oversight are further advantaged in that they are less prone to risk aversion and cautious management than public coping organizations brought about by the bureaucratic inefficiencies that public control over educational production produces.[33]

This is an important distinction, because education contains both public and private coping organizations. While the tasks and difficulties in assessment are present in both schools characterized by monopoly and those characterized by parental choice, the latter have several advantages over the former, notably the incessant threat of exit by customers, whose perceptions of quality are much closer to the ground. When one thinks about private coping organizations in education, one probably first thinks of private schools, which are typically not subject to any of No Child Left Behind's potential sanctions. However, charter schools—publicly funded, semi-autonomous schools started by teachers, parents, and community activists—are also subject to the choices of their customers. However, charter schools are public schools, subject to the same testing and sanctioning under No Child Left Behind as traditional public schools. I will take up the issue of charter schools in detail in chapter 4.

To go a bit beyond Wilson's definition of coping organizations, schools might be a relatively rare but theoretically interesting subset of coping organizations. I call these "experiential organizations," since experience defines nearly everything about what the organization does, how well it does it, how one can or cannot measure its quality, and the effects of measurement on quality. The term comes from the work of John Dewey, who early in the twentieth century foreshadowed the subsequent debate over the most important determinants of educational quality: "The history of educational theory is marked by opposition between the idea that education is development from within and that it is formation from without."[34] In Dewey's analysis, Wilson's distinction between outputs and outcomes might be thought of as two sides of the same problem of experience. What schools do and how they do it represent the same fleeting and possibly unmeasurable agglomeration of lived experiences: "I assume that amid all uncertainties there is one permanent frame of reference: namely, the organic connection between education and personal experience."[35]

The idea of experiential organizations really constitutes only a small modification of Wilson's coping organization framework, and I do not pretend to have developed a new theory here but only to highlight some interesting characteristics of schools as a special subset of these organizations. The primary difference between experiential organizations and other types of coping organizations is the degree to which experiential organizations are subject to the challenges of congestion effects. While, as Wilson observes, schools' tasks define much about their organization and operation, the fact that the quality of education is coproduced by students and their peers leads to a critical role for the social context of production. The degree to which principals and teachers foster or do not foster a climate of high expectations and student engagement is critical to whether quality will be produced. In education, tasks undoubtedly matter, but school culture may matter just as much.[36]

The second distinction between schools and other types of coping organizations is the way that experience has cumulative effects on quality. No student is ever really on a level playing field. Given that experience has cumulative effects on education, schools have increasing difficulty raising achievement as a student moves through the grades. Another implication is that resources, properly applied, are much more critical for students whose lived experiences reflect a lifetime of economic deprivation. This alone may render arguments that money does not matter in education theoretically unsound and may support the idea of spending significantly more on educating the poorest children than the wealthiest parents are willing to spend on educating their own.

I also disagree with Wilson's assertion that managers and operators, principals and teachers will always be in opposition to each other. Though likely true in coping organizations, it is not as clear that this proposition holds in experiential organizations. Given the importance of school culture in producing quality education, the best way for principals to control their teachers is to select the best teachers available, support them as much as possible, and let them do their jobs without too much interference. Educational reforms need to include the premise that the importance of context and culture renders micromanagement and conflict-driven leadership counter-productive.

In education, the product itself is an experience whose quality depends on a life history composed of many experiences. The conditions of production matter critically to the quality of the experience provided. Our measures will themselves change educational production, as principals and teachers shift their production to focus on measurable outcomes. We cannot understand how to reform schools without also realizing that we will always be dealing with a set of largely unobservable, perhaps unmeasurable, and always ephemeral experiences.

Few types of organizations fit the descriptions of coping organizations (or my experiential subset of them). One might think that health care would fit the bill; however, more tangible measures of success and failure ultimately exist in spite of the fact that outputs are typically unobserved except by patient and provider. Physicians are not held responsible for failing to get their patients to stop smoking, but schools are held responsible for failing to get their students to stop disrupting the class. The best—perhaps only—example of an experiential organization outside of education is religious institutions. The interface between the individual and the services of a church, mosque, synagogue, or temple is as difficult to observe as that between a student and a school. The outcomes are more or less impossible to quantify. Congestion effects, recipient engagement, and cumulative experience all factor into whether the individual attains the religious organization's spiritual goals. Of course, we do not regulate religious organizations with anywhere near the zeal with which we regulate schools, and the federal government has never devised an initiative called No Souls Left Behind. However, the analogy highlights just how ephemeral "educational quality" is.

This somewhat lengthy digression allows for a deeper understanding of the underlying challenges of No Child Left Behind and provides the ability to make some theoretically grounded predictions about how it is going to play out. I will conclude by summarizing what I have learned about experiential organizations and what this understanding can tell us about how No Child Left Behind will work and how it might be made to work better.

1. The methods of measurement will determine the quality that one observes.

Cross-sectional objective measures of educational performance capture mostly things over which a school has no control but that impact observed quality, such as the student's ability, his or her achievement at the time of testing, his or her current peer groups, the total value of all educational services received up to that point, parental involvement, and a nontrivial amount of noise. Unless it is modified, No Child Left Behind will do an excellent job of identifying and sanctioning schools that fail to be rich and of majority ethnicity. This phenomenon results partly from to the use of cross-sectional tests whose results capture mostly phenomena over which a school has no control, especially resource inequalities between schools and students. Under top-down sanction, schools that enroll larger numbers of students whose experiences involve the factors that make for lower achievement will be disproportionately identified and punished. Assessment models that base their measurements on gains in student achievement will do a better job of identifying schools that are producing educational quality; however, the process will remain indirect and uncertain.

2. Leadership matters, but it does not dominate student experience.

Effective leadership creates the conditions under which quality is produced but cannot always compensate for all of the lived experiences of the students before they enroll in a particular grade or school or outside of the school walls. To the extent that schools serve traditionally underperforming students, under the current model of AYP identification and sanction, they will be disproportionately identified as failing, regardless of how well they are really doing. Since charter schools typically serve students in lower-income communities, NCLB will also fall very hard on one of its potential solutions for reconstituting chronically underperforming schools: the charter school. Policymakers' remaining options, such as firing the entire staff or contracting out for private management, will be much more contentious and controversial.

   3. Quality in education is a group effort, and those closest to
      the educational production process are best able to assess
      its quality.

Educational quality is coproduced—by the receivers of the services (students, peer groups of students, and parents) and the deliverers of those services (the schools, teachers, and administrative and governmental agencies)—within a specific context that exerts its own influences on production. Quality depends on the experiences that principals create in the schools, the experiences that teachers create in the classroom, the lives of students within and outside of the school, and the degree to which peers reinforce or hinder the teachers' efforts. School culture, therefore, becomes both an indicator of and a factor in school success

Reforms aimed at aligning the interests of schools and customers have the potential to produce a truer measure of educational quality than top-down sanctioning and, therefore, a more quality-focused management. It is to be hoped that these two strategies will overlap, but they are not necessarily equal in their ability to find true quality, nor are they necessarily coincident in their determinations about whether that quality is present. There is no theoretical reason why regular public schools would not benefit from an incentive structure that required paying close attention to parental evaluations of quality and rewarded these efforts with increased bureaucratic autonomy and perhaps financial resources. In fact, the theory quite clearly indicates that traditional public schools should be allowed to operate under such an incentive structure.

   4. The act of measuring quality impacts the production
      process.

Reform efforts will change the production process in schools— for better or worse—as school managers orient themselves to the assessment regimen in place. Therefore, school managers will respond to test-based assessment by trying to increase test scores and to choice- based assessment by trying to improve the school-customer relationship. NCLB will produce precisely the kinds of behaviors and attitudes on the part of public school administrators that make excellence in management less rather than more likely. Attitudes and behaviors associated with mission orientation, risk taking, and programmatic improvement are more likely to be found in public school principals facing competition from charter schools than those operating under the threat of state sanction, controlling for other influences on leadership and student performance.

If we are serious about making accountability work, then we need to consider looking more directly at the performance of the school's managers and operators—which is, after all, what we are trying to change—in a system that adds meaningful rewards to the menu of punishments embodied in the legislation. Policymakers should consider looking beyond any variant of a standardized-testing model as the only objective measure of high-quality educational production. With these conclusions, suggestions, and predictions in mind, I now turn to empirical analyses. By getting back to the basics of educational quality, the rest of this exploration will provide at least a rough guide to what we can expect to see as we progress through No Child Left Behind's peculiar world and will offer some tangible ideas for how to achieve its liberal promises.

CHAPTER 3

Making the Grade (or Not)

Success and Failure in NCLB's World

> Gaps in school achievement, as measured, for example,
> in the eighth grade, have deep roots—deep in out of
> school experiences and deep in the structures of schools.
> Inequality is like an unwanted guest who comes early and
> stays late.
>
> *Paul E. Barton,* Parsing the Achievement Gap

On a cool August day at the 2003 Minnesota State Fair, Republican governor Tim Pawlenty helped a South St. Paul fifth-grader named Jeremy look up his school's brand-new report card on the Internet. Calling the program Accountability on a Stick—in reference to the fact that people attending the Minnesota State Fair can find almost anything fried and stuck on a stick—Pawlenty praised the report cards and the positive effects that they would have on accountability for Minnesota's public schools:

> Traditionally, the measure of our commitment to schools has always been just, "How much are we spending?" That's a good and important measure, but it's an incomplete measure. We also want the measurement to be, "What are we getting for the

money? What are we getting in terms of student learning and performance and accountability?"[1]

The report card for Jeremy's elementary school included summaries of student test scores, demographics, teacher qualifications, and—at the centerpiece of the initiative—a rating of between one (worst) and five (best) stars.

The foundation for these star ratings—fulfilling No Child Left Behind's requirement to publicize achievement—was a school's success or failure to make adequate yearly progress (AYP).[2] In this, the system's first year, only elementary and combined elementary/middle schools were rated. Stars were assigned in both reading and math, based on the results of third- and fifth-grade achievement tests. For the ratings, schools were compared to other, similar schools based on size and percentage of students qualifying for free or reduced-price lunch. The star ratings were normalized, meaning that only the top performing schools within similar comparison groups could attain the highest ratings. Schools that failed to make AYP in any area could do no better than two stars, regardless of how well they did on the test results for any other grade or subgroup.

In this pilot year, Jeremy's South St. Paul School received three stars, as did the vast majority of Minnesota's elementary schools. This pattern held true the following year, when middle and high schools were incorporated into ratings system. The result was largely by design, since high ratings were awarded on a competitive basis. "Schools," noted the president of the Minnesota teachers' union, "are graded on a curve, and therefore it would be statistically impossible for every school to perform at the top."[3] Even in Minnesota, not all schools are allowed to be above average.

In many other ways, Jeremy's school was average as well. It enrolled roughly the same percentage of white students (84 percent) as Minnesota's public schools as a whole (81 percent), slightly fewer African American students, and slightly more Hispanic students. Just under a third of the students were eligible for free or reduced-price lunch, slightly higher than the state average.

So why did Jeremy's school receive only an average rating? His school might have represented a snapshot of average Minnesota, with its test scores reflecting more Jeremy's peers and the level of community resources than anything that the schools were or were not doing. It could also be that Jeremy's teachers and principals have been performing up to a decent standard, but nothing more. Or, it could be neither of these, or some of both. The ratings offer little guidance, especially for those schools that failed to make AYP and therefore received no more than two stars. Given the critical role played by student and community characteristics in educational production (as discussed in chapter 2), it is very difficult to extract the performance of any school from the sociodemographic characteristics of its student body. This is equally true in looking at test scores, success or failure to make AYP, or any list of "blue ribbon" schools based on the results of a state's standardized tests.

This chapter begins the book's empirical analyses, offering a detailed look at the relationships among community characteristics, school leadership, and the specific testing provisions of No Child Left Behind. I focus on AYP as it relates to school and student characteristics and the patterns of leadership among public school principals. The questions for this chapter are

Why do schools succeed or fail to make AYP?
Given the dominance of ethnicity and resource inequality in determining achievement test scores, do school principals' actions matter at all to measured educational achievement?

No Child Left Behind in State and Nation

The details of implementation in the world of No Child Left Behind constitute a somewhat unique and often contentious result of a process of bargaining between state and federal education officials.[4] Though states devise and implement their own plans, these plans are structured by the law and must be approved by the U.S. Department of Education. There are three main areas where state policies and context can shape the number of schools that make or fail to make AYP. The first is the underlying rigor of the tests used in these assessments, which are likely based on accountability measures already in use prior to NCLB's passage. The second is the decision regarding where to set the minimum cutoff point for separate evaluation of students of nonmajority ethnicity, those with limited English proficiency, and those with special education needs, along with related questions of whether to use confidence intervals and other techniques to smooth out the data. The third is the composition of the student bodies across states and communities, especially the relative percentages of a state's students that qualify for separate evaluation under NCLB's rules. Some of these factors fall under the states' control; some do not.

The variation among state plans resulting from this negotiated interface in the law's implementation presents an interesting challenge for researchers. Focusing on interstate differences in these details to explain patterns of school success and failure risks aggregating data that may not be meaningfully comparable. Yet ignoring interstate differences can lead to a narrow focus, particularly if one is examining the relationship between these particular provisions of the law and its ultimate success or failure.[5] What is needed is a body of research that addresses the ways in which state choices about NCLB specifics impact school outcomes but that also includes a more focused analysis of how the commonalities of the challenges of measuring achievement confront school principals, teachers, and education officials across states.

This book takes the second approach: raising and exploring the challenges of defining and identifying educational quality in a specific context—particularly using any standardized measures of achievement—and using these evaluations to make specific suggestions about how to make the law work better. In this approach, interstate differences in the details of NCLB implementation will not be the key factor in NCLB's success or failure. Rather, NCLB will likely stand or fall on the degree to which the framework of the national policy does or does not consider the core challenge of measuring what is good in education. This question has not been sufficiently addressed in all of the debate about NCLB. If the findings in this book are useful, then a next step might be a cross-state comparison of the patterns that emerge in this more focused study.

To do this, I combine what we currently know about how NCLB is playing out in the country with an extensive analysis of original data from one state, Minnesota. Though most of this book's data for empirical analysis come from one state, this book is not really about Minnesota but rather about key issues that are playing out or are likely to play out across the country. I combine the in-depth exploration of the data from Minnesota with information about what others have found relating to other cities and states, thereby providing a window onto a very complex phenomenon.

Focusing on the on-the-ground effects of No Child Left Behind in Minnesota in particular offers several advantages. First, the state is an early and active adopter of NCLB's provisions, making it a better case for finding positive benefits from NCLB than states that do not consistently comply with law. Compared to other states, it has been a leader in compliance and implementation of No Child Left Behind.[6] Minnesota also often receives praise for having high-quality schools, traditionally scoring quite high in state-to-state comparisons of national test scores. Thus, looking at what Minnesota's school leaders think about NCLB and at how they are responding to the law offers a sort of best-case scenario for high-stakes testing and accountability.

The empirical data for most of this book combine the results of the Minnesota Schools Survey, an original survey of 1,434 Minnesota public and charter school principals conducted in the fall of 2003, with the results of follow-up interviews conducted shortly thereafter.[7] Survey questionnaires were sent to all public and charter school principals in Minnesota in November and December 2003.[8] I followed up these surveys with e-mail interviews of a small but diverse group of survey respondents.[9] While I do not attempt to draw any broad conclusions from these follow-up interviews, the responses are useful for adding some detail to the comprehensive survey results and at times complicate, challenge, or contextualize the results of the empirical tests. I will draw on the interview results for these more limited purposes.

Though Minnesota lacks a high concentration of students of minority ethnicity, the state offers the chance to combine analyses of diverse urban settings, less diverse suburban settings, and rural settings, which are often omitted from educational policy analysis. Finally, the state's moderate size allowed me to conduct a survey (a census, actually) of all of the state's public school principals. Such a comprehensive survey, combined with the high response rate, allows greater confidence in the observed patterns than might otherwise be possible.

Of course, the data for this study come from only one state—not coincidentally, the one in which I live. The question arises, in the vocabulary of political science, of generalizability—that is, the degree to which studies in one specific context provide information about what will happen in different contexts. Minnesota exhibits some notable differences from most other states. In addition to its academic excellence, Minnesota ranks at or near the top of the nation in measures of all sorts of good, civic-minded behaviors and attitudes. To paraphrase the framing of social capital theorist Robert Putnam, Minnesotans bowl together.[10] Does Minnesota's status as a state that features high social capital in any way narrow the broader utility of my findings?

I would answer no, although my data do not permit a definitive response to the question. The state's high levels of civic involvement seem likely to lead to more participation in education than in other states. If so, then the danger of reallocating principals' attention away from parents and toward test scores may be less destructive in Minnesota than in states starting out with lower levels of trust and involvement. Fundamentally, however, this book examines the effects of No Child Left Behind on individual principals confronting the challenges posed by uncertainty and limited time across all states, not how the details of state policies will condition these responses.

While, for example, the intensity of the responses of school principals to the threat of sanction may be shaped by how high a state sets the bar for achieving AYP, what method or combination of methods the state uses, or how vigorously the state pursues the sanctions for underperforming schools, the fundamental challenge of measuring educational quality is present in every school in each of the states. Given the considerable variation in states' definitions of proficiency, it may not make much sense to place too much faith in cross-state comparisons of No Child Left Behind's effects. With the stakes involved in NCLB's success or failure as high as they are, it is, therefore, it is not a bad idea to establish whether these themes matter at all in one state before comparing the specific consequences of NCLB on the patterns of principals' leadership.

Like the rest of the country, Minnesota has witnessed a persistent and growing disparity in the test scores of students of majority and nonmajority ethnicities and from advantaged and disadvantaged homes. A 2002 study by the University of Minnesota's Office of Educational Accountability found some hopeful evidence that gaps between minority and nonminority students were narrowing a bit; nevertheless, these gaps remained quite large. Moreover, the gaps between economically advantaged and disadvantaged students appeared to be widening.[11] In the face of these inequalities, the Minnesota Department of Education framed its response to No Child Left Behind specifically in terms of remedying this problem: "This accountability system will help Minnesota solve the biggest challenge it faces in education: closing the achievement gaps between students of color and white students."[12]

The heart of Minnesota's implementation plan is a home-grown, previously existing test: the Minnesota Comprehensive Assessments. The Minnesota Comprehensive Assessments were not the only tests used in the state prior to 2002, nor were they originally designed to test students in grades three through eight and again in high school, as NCLB demands. Like many other states, Minnesota entered the No Child Left Behind era with multiple tests, shifting and politically contentious content standards (particularly in social studies), and the need to significantly ramp up testing and scoring capacity to meet the new federal demands.

As No Child Left Behind requires, Minnesota evaluates schools in four areas: test participation, test proficiency, average daily attendance, and (for high schools) graduation rates. Schools must demonstrate that 95 percent of their students took the test for all of their students and for any of the eight subgroups for which the school has a large enough population to trigger the evaluation (a number that the state generally sets at forty).[13] These participation rules were designed to prevent schools from encouraging low-performing students to stay home on test day. While these rules discourage cheating, they raise their own problems, particularly with the possibility that a school could be labeled as failing if one student in one sub-group stayed home on test day.[14]

Rather than looking at the total number of students attaining a proficiency threshold, Minnesota assigns points to schools based on the level of proficiency demonstrated according to a five-point scale. Schools receive no points for students achieving "significantly below grade level," half a point for students "approaching grade level performance," and one point for each student who demonstrates "grade level performance or above."[15] In addition, each elementary or middle school was required to demonstrate a 90 percent average daily attendance rate, not broken down by subgroups, and each high school had to demonstrate a 90 percent graduation rate, again not disaggregated. During the 2002–3 school year, Minnesota tested students in grades three and five in reading and math. Middle schools made or failed to make AYP on the basis of their attendance, while high schools were rated on the basis of graduation. In 2003–4, the state added math test results for grades seven and eleven and reading test results for grades seven and ten. For 2003–4, the Minnesota cutoff for subgroups in test proficiency was twenty students for all of the subgroups except special education, where it was forty students.

Not surprisingly, some glitches and concerns have arisen regarding the implementation of No Child Left Behind in Minnesota. Equally unsurprisingly, the state's urban schools are not doing very well: said one observer, "It's generally been just poor urban schools, with a smattering of others, that have been labeled by the state as low-performing because their average test scores on state tests have been too low."[16] While it is too early to tell if achievement scores have sustained across-the-board increases, several concerns are already being discussed. Most of these are related to the rising reading and math proficiency targets. By the 2013–14 school year, every school in Minnesota (and the rest of the country) will have to show that all of its students—and all of its students within qualifying subgroups—have achieved the state's standards.

That deadline and the 100 percent passage requirement worry Minnesota's educators and policymakers for several reasons. The first is cost. Though a 2004 report by the Minnesota Office of the Legislative Auditor—the most comprehensive analysis of NCLB implementation in Minnesota to date—noted that although the costs of implementing the law's requirements had been "modest, so far,"[17] the researchers could not even estimate the costs of compliance with the 100 percent proficiency requirement or of sanctioning all of the schools that failed to meet it.

The second worry is one of perverse incentives. Given the increased probability of AYP failure in larger, more diverse schools, Minnesota's educators and administrators fear that No Child Left Behind will make school principals and district officials reluctant to offer services to high-need students, since parents of such students would be likely, under Minnesota's statewide school-choice program, to gravitate to such schools. The potential for resegregating the schools appears to be another plausible though unintended consequence of the law's implementation.

District superintendents interviewed for the Minnesota Legislative Auditor's study worried about the inevitable trade-offs that would occur: "The biggest challenge with NCLB is the need to reallocate existing resources (staff and operating) to meet requirements. This means that we don't provide some of the other programs that have been in place."[18] The question of trade-offs is important, and I will deal with it at length in the next chapter from the point of view of the school principal. A principal's scarcest and most valuable resource is time. School principals are, in the terminology of political scientists, "boundedly rational,"[19] meaning that principals try to make the best decisions that they can given the competing demands on their time. Principals will make most decisions with a great deal of uncertainty, and they will never have enough time to obtain complete information. The worry, from the point of view of No Child Left Behind, is that principals will be forced to reallocate their time in ways that do not lead to better learning for the students but instead lead to an avoidance of the law's punitive consequences.

Other problems and unintended consequences began to surface as Minnesota moved ahead with implementing its NCLB plan. The first list of underperforming schools, published in July 2003, identified 259 of roughly 1,800 schools as having failed to make AYP. A month later, the Minnesota Department of Education presented a revised list that contained 93 fewer schools.[20] Officials claimed that clerical errors and data problems had resulted in the higher total, but the principals in those 93 schools had a lot of explaining to do during that month. In the winter of 2004, many Minneapolis parents were upset when their children brought home quarter-inch-thick homework packets to be completed over winter break as a means of helping the students perform better on the spring tests.[21] And, in April 2005, several Minnesota districts were forced to ask parents not to participate in Take Your Child to Work Day, which fell during one of the test weeks, imperiling districts and schools under NCLB's test participation requirement.[22]

In the long term, however, Minnesota district superintendents most fear that No Child Left Behind will lead to a wholesale condemnation of the state's public schools. Using simulation techniques based on three scenarios—that Minnesota's public schools will improve academic achievement at a high, medium, or low rate—the 2004 report by the Minnesota Office of the Legislative Auditor (hardly a partisan advocacy group) concluded that by 2014, "most Minnesota schools will not meet NCLB's goals"[23] and that "between 80 and 100 percent of Minnesota elementary schools will fail to make AYP."[24] A superintendent in an increasingly affluent and well-regarded suburban district worried that 90 percent of his district's schools would eventually fail and that his district's experiences would hardly be unique: "There's the fear that in a decade public schools will either disappear or look far, far different from what they do today."[25] If Minnesota's schools, which consistently rank at or near the top if the nation in test-score comparisons, are headed for closure, then the national picture could deteriorate even more dramatically. The country is accelerating very quickly down a road whose contours are not fully understood and whose potholes may be much larger than anyone has imagined.

Casting a Wide and Indiscriminate Net

The best analogy that I can think of when trying to envision the effects of No Child Left Behind on specific schools—in Minnesota or any other state—is that of throwing large nets into the water, letting them drift for a while, and bringing in everything that gets stuck in their weave. The effect of NCLB is drift-net fishing for low quality schools.

If we compare schools based only on the percentages of their students meeting proficiency targets, then we can expect to catch some of what we are hoping to catch: schools that we objectively conclude are not doing well because they really are inefficient or otherwise underperforming. However, many schools wind up in our nets even though we do not want them there. Some of these schools may be doing an adequate job but wind up identified simply because they have diverse or high-need student populations. Given the correlation between a lifetime of resource inequalities and lower academic achievement and given the fact that more diverse schools have more ways to fail to make AYP under NCLB's subgroup rules, large diverse schools are much more likely to fail to make AYP, regardless of what their principals and teachers do. These one- and two-star schools will fail to make AYP only because of all of those factors in educational production that have nothing to do with teachers' and principals' actions and everything to do with the legacy of resource inequalities.

We can also expect to catch a few schools that are actively doing good things but that fail to make AYP only because of the relationship between the way that educational quality is measured and the student population. The teachers and principals in these unlucky schools are actively engaged in the kinds of behaviors that decades of effective schools research have shown matter to academic achievement: involved parents, safe and orderly environments, clear standards, and motivated teachers. But these schools are doing so while serving traditionally underperforming students, hence their misidentification under the current system. The very best of urban and rural public schools, charter schools, and alternative learning environments are particularly at risk for this kind of treatment. These high-quality schools are No Child Left Behind's dolphins.

Of course, this analogy only goes so far. After all, in fishing, the net is not designed to scare fish into changing their types or behaviors, as NCLB is supposed to do, though without much guidance on how this process will happen. The point is that large-scale indiscriminate measurement may be more haphazard or dangerous than is currently imagined. Another unfortunate fishing metaphor hopefully will not prove apt. "Ghost nets" are broken-off pieces of drift nets that float around the ocean, ensnaring creatures and dragging them down to the bottom of the sea. It is not difficult to imagine pieces of No Child Left Behind floating around causing damage long after the law has been scrapped, modified, or left to die from underfunding.

The importance of the relationship between a school's diversity and its prospects under NCLB served as the basis for John R. Novak and Bruce Fuller's conclusion that schools are currently being "dinged for diversity."[26] In their study of school success and failure in California, the authors found that "even when students display almost identical average test scores, schools with more subgroups are more likely to miss their growth targets under federal rules set by the No Child Left behind Act."[27]

Having diverse student populations increases the likelihood of AYP failure for two reasons. The first, as I discussed at length in chapter 2, is that diversity in student populations typically also means resource inequalities, with all of the attendant negative consequences for test score results. The second reason is more prosaic but just as important. As discussed in chapter 1, test score results under NCLB are disaggregated by eight racial, ethnic, and needs subgroups, with thirty-six different ways to fail at each grade level tested if that grade level contains enough students in that subgroup to trigger AYP. The larger and more diverse a school's population, therefore, the higher the chances of failure.

The question of where to set the minimum subgroup size for proficiency and, to a lesser extent, test participation is critical to both the number of schools that fail to make AYP and to a state's commitment to closing the achievement gap between students of minority and nonminority ethnicity—in other words, to whether individual states and the country as a whole live up to NCLB's promises. States vary considerably in setting the minimum number required to trigger academic performance evaluation for groups of minority, limited English proficient (LEP), or special needs students. Cutoff levels range between ten and fifty students, with many states choosing higher levels for special education and LEP students.

State decisions regarding the subgroup cutoff number matter

when they—in their desire to reduce the number of sanctioned schools—attempt to modify these and other provisions of the law. The political and economic costs of large-scale school failures are quite high. As strategic political actors, therefore, state legislatures and departments of education are already trying to modify the rules of assessment to produce a smaller list of failing schools. By 2004, forty-seven states had applied to the U.S. Department of Education "to approve changes to their accountability plans—changes that in many cases make it easier for schools and school districts to show adequate yearly progress."[28] These proposed changes included increases in the minimum subgroup size, exemptions for small schools, and averaging proficiency data over two or more years.

In 2005 in Minnesota, for example, schools were allowed to use one- to three-year averages of test scores rather than the current year only as a means of smoothing out the inevitable bounces in test score results between years. In addition, the academic achievement of LEP students was examined separately only if the schools had at least forty such students in the grade level, twice the cutoff used a year earlier. These two changes alone resulted in the removal of 197 schools from the list of those failing.[29] If the 2004 rules had remained in effect, then what at first appeared to be a tremendous improvement in school quality—a 50 percent drop in the number of failing schools—disappears entirely, making it very difficult to tell whether genuine changes in school quality took place. These kinds of rules changes, with all of their attendant uncertainties, will increase the difficulty of determining whether No Child Left Behind is working.

In spite of the potential importance of minimum subgroup size to AYP compliance in a given school, subgroup cutoff levels alone do not appear to determine what percentage of a state's schools make or fail to make AYP. As figure 4 shows, no clear relationship appears to exist between the percentages of schools in a state that failed to make AYP in 2004 and that state's choice of a minimum number of students for separate AYP evaluation, possibly in part because not all states set the cutoff levels uniformly across groups. However, the primary reason for this finding is that states differ on many other crucial characteristics, including the underlying rigor of the tests and the percentages of minority and low-income students that the state serves.

Figure 5 presents the relationship between a state's percentage of

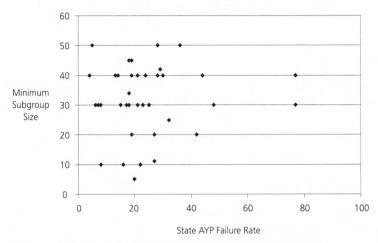

The Relationship between Subgroup Size and State AYP
Failure Rates in the United States, 2004

Fig. 4. Subgroup cutoff rules and state AYP failure rates. (AYP data from National Education Association 2006; minimum subgroup size from Pierce 2003.)

minority students and the percentage of its schools that failed to make AYP in 2004. This relationship is positive and statistically significant. States with more diverse student populations are more likely to have higher percentages of failing schools. Of course, none of these basic analyses account for state-to-state differences in the underlying rigor of the tests. The analyses do suggest, however, that getting at the heart of the opportunities and challenges of No Child Left Behind may require a deep rather than broad look at the many details of assessment under the law.

When assigning quality ratings to schools based only on their aggregate test score data—even when taking the community characteristics partially into account—policymakers run the risk of singling out schools for reasons that have nothing to do with events within the school and classroom walls, a troubling pattern that researchers have found in other states. The concern here, therefore, is the degree to which policymakers can extract the true quality of educational production from a set of aggregate test scores, no matter how carefully obtained.

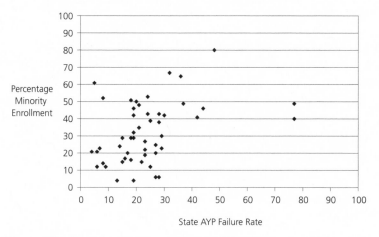

The Relationship between Percentage Minority Enrollment and AYP Failure Rates in the United States, 2004

Fig. 5. Minority student enrollment and state AYP failure rates. (AYP data from National Education Association 2006; demographic data from National School Boards Association 2006.)

Comparing Minnesota's five-star traditional public schools based on their student and teacher characteristics raises concerns similar to what has been observed in California and elsewhere (see table 2, which presents the characteristics of Minnesota's traditional public schools that received five-star ratings in either reading or math in 2004).[30] In 2004, Minnesota's five-star schools typically enrolled half as many minority students as the rest of the schools in the state, 60 percent as many students who qualified for free or reduced-price lunch, and less than a third as many LEP students. Teachers in five-star schools had higher salaries and were more likely than those in the rest of Minnesota's public schools to have master's degrees.

Comparing the student populations of public schools that made AYP in 2004 to those schools that did not make AYP reveals a similarly troubling pattern (table 3). Minnesota's diverse public schools do not fare particularly well under No Child Left Behind. These schools, however, also disproportionately serve students whose demographic characteristics are associated with fewer lifetime resource

inputs—which are critical to true quality in educational production—and lower academic performance. The question, then, is
whether Minnesota's diverse public schools are being singled out
because of their student populations or because of their product's
true quality. Nothing in the current implementation of the No Child
Left Behind legislation allows one to distinguish between schools that
fail to serve their students and a policy that fails to help the schools.

Most Minnesota public elementary schools qualified in two or
fewer subgroup targets in 2003, and most of these schools made AYP.
Larger schools and those with more qualifying categories of students;
however, were significantly more likely to fail to make AYP in both

TABLE 2.   School Characteristics and Minnesota's Five-Star Public Schools, 2004

	Five Star (1)	All Others (2)
Percentage of minority students	9%	19%
Percentage of students eligible for free or reduced-price lunch	15%	25%
Percentage of special education students	11%	13%
Percentage of LEP students	2%	7%
Percentage of teachers with master's degrees	45%	39%
Average teacher salary	$45,043	$44,253
Number of schools (percentage of total)	181 (12%)	1,307 (88%)

Source: Author's analysis based on data from Minnesota Department of Education 2003c, 2004b.

TABLE 3.   Drift-Net Fishing for Low-Quality Schools: No Child Left Behind's Minnesota Catch, 2004

	Public Schools That Made AYP (1)	Public Schools That Failed to Make AYP (2)
Percentage of enrolled students classified as . . .		
Black	4%	15%
Hispanic	4%	8%
American Indian	2%	5%
Asian or Pacific Islander	3%	9%
Eligible for free or reduced-price lunch	21%	35%
LEP	4%	13%
Special education	13%	14%

Source: Author's analysis based on data from Minnesota Department of Education 2003c, 2003d, 2004a.

reading and mathematics proficiency (table A1). Schools that qualified in five or six subgroups failed to make AYP at least 40 percent of
the time, while those schools that qualified in only one category (typically for white, non-Hispanic students) failed less than 1 percent of
the time. It would be very difficult to defend the assertion that the
teachers and principals in affluent communities are better than their
counterparts in poorer communities by a factor of forty or more.

Figure 6 presents these relationships graphically by comparing
the percentages of Minnesota's public schools that failed to make
AYP in 2004 based on the characteristics of their student populations. The patterns of failure in Minnesota's high-need schools are
striking. Nearly half of Minnesota's public schools that qualified in
the top quarter of schools on the basis of high minority, free-lunch-
eligible, and LEP populations failed to make AYP in 2004, more than
twice the state's average failure rate for that year. For schools that
qualified in both high minority and high free-lunch categories, the
failure rate reached 54 percent. As Minnesota and the rest of the
nation expand the number of grades tested, even more of the most
diverse schools are likely to fail. Across the country as in Minnesota,
minority ethnicity and low income tend to go hand in hand. The percentage of students classified as minority and the percentage of students eligible for free or reduced-price lunch are highly correlated.[31]
Add to this the fact that only those public schools eligible to receive
Title I funds (given for aid to low-income students) are subject to
NCLB's increasingly harsh sanctions, and the playing field looks anything but even.

Figure 7 presents the relationship between the percentages of
Minnesota public schools that achieved five-star status or failed to
make AYP in 2004 and the racial and ethnic diversity of their student
populations. Schools are ordered from left to right, divided into
equal increments of seventy-four schools (with roughly 5 percent of
schools in each group). The x-axis depicts the percentages of minority students in each of these twenty groups of schools. The schools on
the right, therefore, contain higher percentages of minority students.
The y-axis presents average percentages of public schools in these
groups that failed to make AYP or were labeled as five-star schools in
2004.

The Percentages of Minnesota's Regular Public Schools Failing to Make AYP, 2004

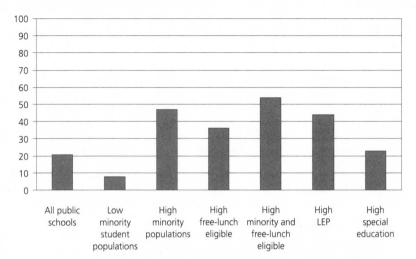

Fig. 6.   **Student composition and AYP failure. (Data are for regular public schools at all grade levels. Quartiles represent between 369 and 372 of the 1,489 regular public schools in the data set [depending on ties in the quartile cutoff]. Data from Minnesota Department of Education 2003c, 2003d, 2004a.)**

The figure demonstrates that the percentage of minority students does not increase evenly in Minnesota's schools, rising slowly at first and then more sharply at the higher end, concentrating high minority populations in a relatively small number of urban and rural schools. The AYP failure rates are much higher for schools with high minority populations, which also have no chance of being labeled as schools of excellence. The same patterns appear when examining the percentages of students eligible for free or reduced-price lunch (figure 8).

The specifics of the patterns of success and failure under No Child Left Behind may be unique to Minnesota and a few other states where diverse student populations are generally confined to urban centers and a few rural communities with large Native American populations. However, the overall picture confirms what other

Minority Student Enrollment, Five-Star Status, and
AYP Failure in Minnesota, 2004

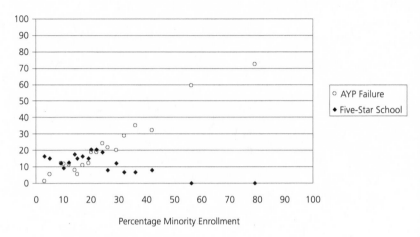

Percentage Minority Enrollment

Fig. 7. Student ethnicity, success, and failure under NCLB. (Data from Minnesota Department of Education 2003c, 2003d, 2004a.)

Free-Lunch Eligible Student Population, Five-Star Status, and
AYP Failure in Minnesota, 2004

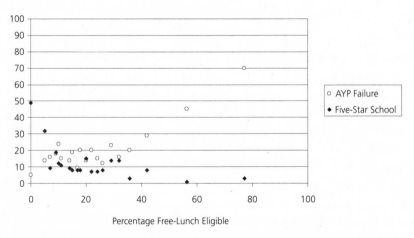

Percentage Free-Lunch Eligible

Fig. 8. Student socioeconomic status, success, and failure under NCLB. (Data from Minnesota Department of Education 2003c, 2003d, 2004a.)

researchers have found in other states—that is, that schools that fail to make AYP are concentrated in racially and ethnically diverse and low-income communities.[32]

Although striking, none of these results allows me to get at my core concern in this chapter: the degree to which these concentrations cause failure or the degree to which they are symptomatic of other underlying factors and processes. In other words, are high-minority and low-income schools, in Minnesota or anywhere else, doomed to one or two stars and AYP identification and sanction under No Child Left Behind, or can teachers and principals make any difference? After all, if we simply look at differences in failure rates between very different schools, we cannot ascertain if a school has failed to make AYP because of the number of categories for which it qualifies, its resource inequalities, or the performance of its teachers and principals. Examining this question requires more complicated techniques.

Leadership, Success, and Failure under No Child Left Behind

The composition of a school's student body clearly matters to success and failure under No Child Left Behind and its snapshot method of evaluating schools. This is hardly a novel finding; however, the magnitude of its influence on outcomes under NCLB is both striking and troubling. If differences in academic achievement result only from student characteristics, then the link between the threat of sanction and improvement in educational quality becomes almost meaningless. As discussed in chapter 2, while achievement tests do appear primarily to capture factors that schools cannot control, several decades of research into schools that work suggest that leadership can matter, at least at the margins.

I will use a measure of how Minnesota school principals spent their time at work to see whether the allocation of time on core or peripheral tasks affects a school's progress under No Child Left Behind. In the fall of 2003, principals were asked, "During the past month, about how much of your time was spent on the following activities?" The activities listed were (1) facilitating the school's mission, (2) supervising faculty, (3) guiding curriculum development,

(4) building relationships with the parent community, (5) maintaining the physical security of students and staff, (6) managing facilities, and (7) completing administrative tasks. The principals reported their answers on a five-point scale, with one the lowest response and five indicating that they spent the most time on that task.

Because the principals self-reported their activities, their responses may have reflected their perceptions of what I wanted to hear. In this case, the emphasis is not on whether principals spend more or less time on one activity or another but on the differences in these reports between schools based on their status under NCLB.

The patterns of principals' allocation of time raise some concerns. The completion of administrative tasks appears to consume far more time than other activities (table A2). Despite the importance of guiding curriculum development, this area appears to receive the least amount of time. These results agree with the findings of those who critique the negative educational consequences of the effects of public bureaucracy.[33] To the extent that No Child Left Behind increases the administrative burdens on principals, it might reduce students' academic achievement or at least counteract any other benefits that the law might produce.

Of the seven areas in which the principals reported their allocation of time, the strongest positive correlations existed between managing facilities and completing administrative tasks on the one hand and focusing on mission, curriculum, and parents on the other. These two groups of variables are negatively correlated with each other, indicating a pattern that makes intuitive sense in how principals cluster their time. These self-reports are included in the analysis to assess whether any association exists between how principals allocate their time during the academic year and the probability that their schools will be identified as failing to make AYP (based on tests administered in the spring) while controlling for students' demographic characteristics.

To disentangle the controllable and uncontrollable factors of achievement and sanction, I conducted a series of multivariate regressions. With roots in the ruminations of observers of eighteenth-century French gamblers, the theory underlying these techniques seeks mostly to tell us how much we do not know and how much faith we can place in what we think we do know. Regression techniques provide some purchase on the magnitude of our uncertainty. In addition, they allow us to disentangle various possible explanations for a phenomenon and to explore other possible causes for observed patterns (see the appendix for tables with these statistical results).

The regression techniques used here have two limitations. First, these or any other statistical techniques at best allow us only to gauge the probability that we are being fooled by our data. We can never know the "truth" but only the probability that the relationships that we see in the data resulted from chance and the randomness inherent in this kind of work. Second, these techniques do not permit me to determine the causal relationship between two factors but only whether they are related. Determining causation requires randomized experiments, which are extraordinarily difficult in education. Few parents would sign up for an experiment that offered a good chance that their children would be placed in low-quality schools.

These techniques can, however, show that one factor is probably related to another factor and is independent of third factor or set of factors. These analyses have as their objective determining whether principals' leadership patterns can make it more or less likely that a school will receive a five-star rating or fail to make AYP based on the test results obtained in the following spring, above and beyond the myriad of student characteristics that we know factor into achievement test scores. In other words, do the best and worst schools in this system differ in their leaders' focus or only in the composition of their student bodies?

I will begin with the mark of success under No Child Left Behind in Minnesota: the five-star school. Five-star status is treated as a function of the demographic characteristics of the student population (including percentage of minority students, percentage of students eligible for free or reduced-price lunch, percentage of LEP students, and percentage of special education students). The model also includes a variable indicating the principal's administrative experience, his or her teaching experience, the school's status as a rural school, the number of students, the highest grade offered in the school, the average teacher salary, the percentage of teachers with master's degrees, and whether the school is a charter school. These same demographic and school variables will be used throughout the analyses.

Most important, the model includes principals' responses to how they spent their time during the previous month.[34] This is the key variable, allowing me to examine whether the ways in which principals allocate their time have any relationship to success under the five-star schools program, independent of all of the other factors that likely affect whether a school is a top scorer on achievement tests.

Other than the negative relationship between percentages of special education students and five-star status, schools are not more or less likely to receive the five-star badge because of their student populations. This makes intuitive sense when one remembers that under Minnesota's plan, schools are compared to those with similar student populations that made AYP. Given the high correlation between student characteristics and AYP failure, student variables would likely be highly significant in a model predicting the probability of being labeled as a one- or two-star school. Schools with higher teachers' salaries appear to be more likely to receive five stars. I will not comment extensively on the teacher variables, though they are included in the models because they are probably important and may be useful for those who would follow up this study.[35]

Figure 9 presents the results of a simulation that uses the coefficient estimates from the underlying probit regression of being labeled a five-star school to produce a set of predicted probabilities that incorporates both principals' self-reported time allocation and the student populations with whom they work.[36] The data portrayed in figure 9 are estimated probabilities rather than actual percentages because the underlying regression techniques are necessary to try to control for those factors that are highly predictive of success on NCLB tests but are unrelated to the behaviors of public school principals. The bars with the dots represent the simulated probabilities that a school will be labeled as a five-star school if that school's principal spent more time on the specific school policy area than 75 percent of his or her colleagues. The solid bars represent the predicted probabilities for those principals who spent less time on the activity than 75 percent of their colleagues at other schools.

These simulations allow me to interpret whether the statistically

Leadership and the Predicted Probability of Being a Five-Star School, 2004

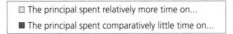

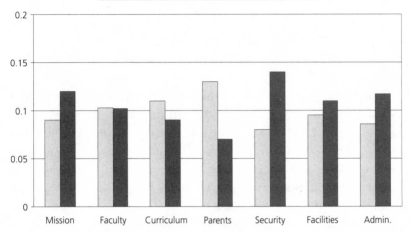

Question:

"During the past month, about how much of your time was spent on the following activities?" Coded: 1 = "None or almost none," 2 = "Slightly less time than on other activities," 3 = "About as much time as other activities," 4 = "Slightly more time than other activities," 5 = "A great deal of time."

Fig. 9. Principals' leadership patterns and success under NCLB. (Probabilities obtained using Clarify [see King, Tomz, and Wittenberg 2000]. *Source:* Minnesota Schools Survey 2003. Demographic, star, and AYP data from Minnesota Department of Education 2003b, 2003c, 2003d, 2004a.)

significant differences that I observed in the regressions are substantively meaningful. They do not provide exact point estimates, as in "Principals who spend a great deal of time reaching out to parents will have a 13 percent chance of having their school receive five stars." Rather, these simulations show the rough magnitude of the effect of principals' behaviors in a way that controls for all of the other things that are known to factor into success on standardized tests.

According to these simulations, principals who focus on reaching out to their parent communities are nearly twice as likely to have their schools labeled as excellent under Minnesota's system. Those who focus instead on security are just under 60 percent as likely to have their schools succeed. The results of the regressions confirm the statistical significance of these differences. Spending more time on curriculum and, somewhat surprisingly, less time on mission are also associated with higher probabilities of success, but these findings are not statistically significant and may result only from the randomness inherent in this kind of research.

That principals in five-star schools spent less time on security is probably not surprising, but it raises an important complication in these analyses. Effective schools research has demonstrated that safe schools are good, but time spent maintaining security is time not spent reaching out to parents or developing and guiding the curriculum. Principals in urban schools likely have to spend more time on security, and they succeed at a lower rate. The danger would be to then assert that having principals spend less time on security causes a school to receive five-star status. This would be a ridiculous and unsupported assertion. Principals do not always control how they spend their time but must always react to events around them. A more critical question is the school's level of safety, orderliness, and security, a point that I will examine in detail in chapter 5.

Figure 10 presents the results of a simulation that examines the other side of Minnesota's compliance with No Child Left Behind: failure to make AYP. As before, the underlying regression estimates are presented in the appendix. Unlike the models of five-star school identification, however, student characteristics matter a great deal to whether a school made or failed to make AYP in 2004, confirming statistically the positive relationship between school diversity and AYP failure. Schools with large minority student populations and those with larger numbers of special education students are twice as likely to fail to make AYP as those with low populations of those two groups. Both of these differences are statistically significant.

An important and significant association also appears to exist between the allocation of principals' time and whether their schools pass or fail the spring round of tests. Mission-oriented principals and those who spent relatively more time guiding the curriculum were more likely to make AYP the following year, while those who were

Probability that a school made AYP in 2004 if...

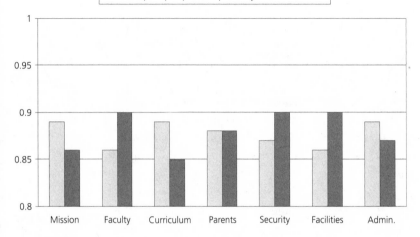

Question:

"During the past month, about how much of <u>your time</u> was spent on the following activities?" Coded: 1 = "None or almost none," 2 = "Slightly less time than on other activities," 3 = "About as much time as other activities," 4 = "Slightly more time than other activities," 5 = "A great deal of time."

Fig. 10. Principals' leadership patterns and failure under NCLB. (Probabilities obtained using Clarify [see King, Tomz, and Wittenberg 2000]. *Source:* **Minnesota Schools Survey 2003. Demographic, star, and AYP data from Minnesota Department of Education 2003b, 2003c, 2003d, 2004a.)**

more focused on managing facilities were more likely to fail to make AYP. While devoting more time to building parent relationships does not appear to be meaningfully associated with a lower probability of AYP failure, spending more time guiding the curriculum and less time managing facilities does appear to pay off.[37] Both of these relationships are statistically significant. Of course, these kinds of survey results cannot establish causation or rule out the possibility that these patterns arise as a consequence of other unobserved variables. However, these results are consistent with what we know about effective schools and principal leadership.[38]

One concern with these results is the possibility that Minnesota's public school principals in high-need schools are failing not because of the legacy of the resource inequalities that they face but because they do not or cannot allocate their time as efficiently. Comparing the allocation of time by principals in high-minority schools with those with smaller minority student populations, however, casts some doubt on this possibility (table A3). Principals in schools with the largest percentages of minority students were more likely to report that they spent a "great deal of time" focused on the school's mission and on reaching out to their parents than principals of low-minority schools. These principals were doing more of what we want them to do with a less active parent community and in the face of serious obstacles to their success under AYP's one-size-fits-all philosophy.[39]

These principals appear, however, to spend more time supervising their faculty, suggesting the possibility that they have less confidence in their teachers' ability to achieve the school's goals without supervision, a long-standing criticism of urban education in this country. Perhaps these principals would have more favorable views of a modified version of No Child Left Behind that more closely based its assessments on actual leadership and that provided principals with more authority to hire and retain the best possible teachers.

Conclusions

In this chapter, I have confirmed in the specific case of No Child Left Behind and the public school principalship what others have observed about academic achievement in general: a lifetime of resource inequalities matters, but leadership can matter, too. With regard to the test scores by which schools are judged, public school principals appear to operate at the margins. However, as Stanley Kelley Jr. observed about elections and Walter Murphy noted about U.S. Supreme Court justices, being able to successfully operate at the margins, "as every student of politics—academic and practical—knows, is saying quite a bit."[40]

I have looked at the effects of leadership on success and failure under No Child Left Behind's particular and possibly peculiar testing strategy. In the next chapter, I will turn to the effects of No Child Left

Behind on principals' influence and leadership decisions. This turn represents a bit of a detour, as I consider the mostly overlooked fact that No Child Left Behind is not the only game in town. Rather, we are simultaneously implementing a set of reforms that seek to control principals and teachers from the top down (in the form of NCLB) and from the bottom up (in the form of charter schools and other forms of school choice). The question is whether these two seemingly contradictory approaches can coexist within the same educational policy space.

CHAPTER 4

Top-Down and Bottom-Up

NCLB, Charter Schools, and the
Public School Principalship

> [We] have only vague notions as to what constitutes
> an educated child or an adequate shelter. But we can
> learn rather easily whether we have satisfied people,
> for the essence of a market is the opportunity it
> affords clients to vote with their feet.
>
> *James Q. Wilson,* Bureaucracy

Accountability systems based on cross-sectional test score results tell us much more about the race, ethnicity, and resource inequalities of students than about the underlying quality of the schooling. But it is also true that leadership can matter to academic achievement, even when measured with an instrument as blunt as aggregate test scores. In this chapter, I will flip the analysis around and look at the effects of No Child Left Behind on leadership rather than the effects of leadership on status under NCLB. To do so, however, I must complicate the picture a bit.

Looking thoroughly at NCLB's effects on leadership within the public schools requires acknowledging that we are simultaneously undertaking the centralized reforms of NCLB and decentralized or consumer-oriented reforms in the form of school choice. The accountability approach underlying NCLB asserts that centralizing and controlling the establishment and enforcement of objective measures of educational quality will allow us to find underperforming schools, help them get better, and spur other schools to improve as a result of this threat. In contrast, school choice policies seek to allow customers to identify schools that are not producing high-quality educational services and to sanction these underperforming schools through the consequences of their departure.

The forms of choice—charter schools, vouchers, and systems of public choice—differ in many important ways, particularly in their effects on political participation;[1] however, they all share the assumption that devolving the power of sanction in educational production as closely as possible to the level of the consumer-client will lead to higher-quality educational services. Customers will choose better schools, and the threat of customer exit will assert a powerful motivational force on all involved in educational production.[2]

While allowing parents of failing schools to use taxpayer-funded vouchers to attend private schools had been part of the original bill, No Child Left Behind as enacted contained no such provisions.[3] Giving parents in failing schools the option of choosing a successful public school, however, survived the law's negotiations and comes into play early in the sanctioning process. NCLB also incorporated a third type of choice, charter schools. These publicly funded but more autonomous schools aim to improve public education by leaving the sanctioning to parents and students in the form of deciding to leave (along with their tax dollars) a traditional public school for a more autonomous (though still public) charter institution. Their autonomy is incomplete, as charter schools are still subject to many regulations, particularly regarding nondiscrimination, health, and safety. They do, however, typically have more freedom in terms of curriculum selection and staff policy than their traditional public counterparts.

Charter schools occupy an interesting position as both targets and solutions under No Child Left Behind. They are subject to the same tests and sanctions as traditional public schools yet are also one of the options for reconstituting a failing school in the later stages of NCLB implementation. In spite of charters' involvement with both top-down and bottom-up reforms, however, the empirical literature has largely ignored their placement as such.[4]

Although charter schools predate the passage of NCLB by a decade, no clear consensus exists about whether charter schools produce better educational quality for their students,[5] though parents appear to be satisfied with their choices.[6] Unfortunately, charter schools' prospects under No Child Left Behind do not appear very promising. Across the country, charter schools appear to be failing to make adequate yearly progress (AYP) at a higher rate than the traditional public schools. In spite of these concerns, the number of charter schools and students who attend them continue to grow, with roughly thirty-four hundred charter schools serving about 1 million students.[7]

Comparing test scores of charter schools and noncharter schools may not be particularly instructive, however, since the lack of demonstrated achievement gains may result mainly from the fact that charter schools often serve student populations with traditionally low academic performance. Given the close and positive relationship between student characteristics and AYP failure rates, it likely matters to charters' disproportionate AYP identification that 42 percent of charter schools are located in only three states—Arizona, California, and Florida—all of which land in the top ten in the United States in terms of percentage minority student enrollment; that roughly half of all charter schools are located in urban centers, compared to 29 percent of regular public schools;[8] and that nearly 60 percent of charter school students are minorities, as opposed to 44 percent of the students in traditional public schools.[9] These patterns are repeated in Minnesota's charter schools, with AYP failure rates more than twice those of traditional public schools but student populations that are much more diverse than those in Minnesota's typical public school (table 4).

The large increase in failure rates among both types of schools results from the growth in the number of grades tested between 2003 and 2004. AYP status in 2003 was based on the results of reading and math tests for grades three and five in elementary schools, attendance by total student population and by subgroups for middle schools, and graduation for high schools. The 2004 AYP calculations also included the results of seventh-grade reading and math tests as well as the results of tenth-grade reading and eleventh-grade math tests.[10] This increase in NCLB's scope will only continue as new grade-level tests are added each year.

Surprisingly, the question of how No Child Left Behind will interact with school choice reforms has received little attention in the literature. Proponents of government-based reforms and advocates of market-based reforms have generally not accounted for the possibility that their approach might not be the only one adopted, though there have been a few exceptions. Political scientist Terry Moe has argued that "a combination of top-down and bottom-up approaches is likely to prove far more potent" than standards-based accountability alone.[11] Chester E. Finn Jr. also argues for the benefits of both approaches simultaneously, calling for a "public policy pluralism" involving standards and choice.[12] Tom Loveless is one of the few

TABLE 4. Minnesota's Charter Schools and No Child Left Behind

	Regular Public Schools (1)	Charter Schools (2)
Percentage of Minnesota schools *not making* adequate yearly progress		
2003	5%	19%
2004	21%	47%
Percentage of enrolled students classified as . . .		
Black	6%	24%
Hispanic	5%	7%
American Indian	3%	5%
Asian or Pacific Islander	4%	7%
Eligible for free or reduced-price lunch	24%	44%
LEP	6%	11%
Special education	13%	14%
Number of schools (2004)	1,589	108

Source: Author's analysis based on data from Minnesota Department of Education 2003b, 2003c, 2003d, 2004a.

Note: The slight discrepancy between some of these calculated percentages and totals and the official figures released by the Minnesota Department of Education results from the exclusion of schools that were missing data on other variables in my subsequent analysis (2.3 percent of the original cases). However, no internal discrepancies exist in subsequent analyses, so these data will be used throughout. Though these data are publicly available, they are used with the verbal permission of the Minnesota Department of Education.

researchers specifically to examine the position of charter schools under No Child Left Behind, noting that studies of their academic achievement gains are not yet conclusive but cautioning that "the number of charters brought under the scrutiny of state accountability systems is certain to increase dramatically" as more grades are brought into No Child Left Behind's assessment system.[13]

Researchers have not yet sufficiently commented on the contradiction inherent in applying a top-down system of accountability to a unique set of public schools whose explicit purpose is to succeed by virtue of their relative freedom from regulation. In spite of their differences, both No Child Left Behind and school choice adopt an indirect approach to improving the quality of schooling. Both approaches are based on the hope that turning the screws, either from above (with NCLB's threat of sanction) or below (with the departure of customers to greener pastures), will induce more quality-oriented behaviors on the part of teachers and administrators.

The underlying theoretical arguments about how these issues have been framed in the policy debate surrounding NCLB have two limitations. First, NCLB makes no effort to encourage principals and teachers to excel in their jobs rather than just shirk. As the discussion of agency in chapter 2 noted, the challenge was to induce the school principal to orient her behavior toward producing higher-quality education. Unfortunately, economists have a difficult time quantifying a person's decision to go above and beyond the call of duty. Rather, school principals or teachers are generally viewed as having three choices: to do their jobs, to slack off (called shirking in the political science literature), or actively to undermine the organization's goals.[14] All else being equal, it is assumed that people will choose to slack off. No room is made for the possibility that a teacher or principal will put in long hours, often at the expense of their private lives, simply because it is the right thing to do.[15]

The second limitation of NCLB's approach is that it fails to take into account the fact that school principals are "boundedly rational," meaning that they make rational decisions but do so in the presence of inevitable limitations on their time and information.[16] The public school principalship is characterized by a great deal of uncertainty and inevitable trade-offs. The problem is that any system of reform, top-down or bottom-up, is likely to lead—for better or worse—to a reorientation of principals' and teachers' time and attention, a problem known in economics as multitasking: "compensation on any subset of tasks will result in a reallocation of activities toward those that are directly compensated and away from the uncompensated activities."[17] While the literature has featured considerable discussion about whether No Child Left Behind will cause teachers to teach to the tests, not enough attention has been paid to the equal possibility that principals will lead to the tests.

Assessing either top-down or bottom-up reforms, economists might ask, "Does this reform keep teachers and principals from shirking?" While this kind of logic makes for nice, tidy economic models, it misses several aspects of educational leadership. Instead, we should be asking whether top-down or bottom-up reforms encourage teachers and principals to go above and beyond the call of duty or whether these reforms will inhibit their ability to do so. We also need to ask how either reform effort might impact the inevitable trade-offs in allocation of time and energy that these people must make every day.

A useful way to think about the decision to excel (rather than to just put in the time) is that of a decision tree. At any step, the possibility for teachers or principals to excel can vanish: only if they make it through all of the steps will they put in the kind of extraordinary effort that will make an impact on students' lives. The principal must care enough to want to try. She must have the autonomy to make meaningful changes. She must have the resources and support to do so. The principal must also have meaningful feedback on whether these efforts are working, and she must be operating under an accountability system that does not ignore or punish her efforts to excel.

This kind of thinking offers some additional context for comparing No Child Left Behind to charter schools and other forms of school choice by raising some important issues to guide further empirical exploration. Specifically, we need to examine whether these two accountability regimes "see" quality in the same way. In other words, customers may perceive schools with higher test scores as more desirable or may look instead for other qualities. In addition, it is important carefully to examine the incentive effects of top-down and bottom-up reforms. The analyses in this chapter explore these questions and potential contradictions in some detail:

What do public school principals think about No Child Left Behind?

What effects does the law have on leadership within the public schools?

What does it mean for the quality of the public school principalship of doing top-down accountability and bottom-up school choice at the same time? Do they reinforce each other, or do they get in each other's way?

Is sanction better than competition?

No Child Left Behind: What Principals Think

Surprisingly, relatively little systematic evidence documents what school principals think about No Child Left Behind and how the law does or does not change the principalship. One of the most comprehensive surveys of leadership under No Child Left Behind was conducted by Public Agenda in 2003.[18] The nearly one thousand public school principals and just over one thousand district superintendents surveyed in Public Agenda's national sample did not report a sense of panic or pessimism but did voice several concerns.[19] In fact, the majority of these school and district leaders felt that insufficient funding, not No Child Left Behind, was their biggest challenge going forward, though NCLB ranked second. More than 80 percent of the superintendents and principals believed that "keeping up with the entire local, state, and federal mandates handed down to the schools takes up way too much time."[20] Nearly three-quarters of district superintendents but less than half of the principals in the study agreed that it is a "good idea to hold principals accountable for students' standardized test scores at the building level."[21] Both sets of school leaders overwhelmingly agreed that "the push for standards, testing, and accountability . . . is something that is here to stay."[22] Both principals and superintendents rejected the idea that No Child Left Behind was irretrievably broken, though they acknowledged that it would "require many adjustments before it can work."[23]

Minnesota's public and charter school principals agreed with the cautious optimism of their counterparts in other states. Though a majority of Minnesota's principals believed that No Child Left Behind would ultimately improve academic achievement, their attitudes suggested some interesting differences (table A6). Principals in regular public schools with large percentages of minority students were more likely to believe that NCLB would improve achievement, and nearly as many principals in schools with large percentages of students eligible for free or reduced-price lunch concurred in spite of the fact that their schools are being placed on the consequences track at a much higher rate than other schools. Principals in charter schools were much less optimistic about NCLB's likely effects, with just over a third believing that it would improve achievement.

Several possible explanations can account for why principals and superintendents have at least some hope for No Child Left Behind. These data do not permit any of these explanations to be completely ruled in or out, but the findings raise some important considerations in thinking about NCLB's prospects. The first possibility is that public school principals think No Child Left Behind is well designed and will work smoothly. Public Agenda's national survey results cast doubt on this assertion. Another possibility involves a question of agency. The threat of sanction can be useful in a principal's hands if it is based on good data and if it improves the ability of good leaders to shape the delivery of educational services in a useful way. Thinking about the law in terms of agency suggests the possibility that top-down accountability might work—alone or in combination with bottom-up reforms—but that the specific provisions and features of No Child Left Behind might provide the wrong mechanism or basis for these evaluations.[24] Finally, there exists the possibility of desperation or least a willingness to live with NCLB's imperfections if doing so will call attention to and perhaps improve the educational conditions in the poorest U.S. communities.

More pessimism generally existed among the small group of Minnesota's principals whom I interviewed about No Child Left Behind's prospects than the larger survey results would indicate. This finding is not surprising, given that those with strong beliefs probably had more incentive to respond to my interview requests, and should not be taken as representative of any underlying distribution of opinions. The details of their concerns, however, are noteworthy. Feelings that NCLB's good intentions will flounder on its improper design centered on a now-familiar litany of concerns. The principal of a small rural elementary school that has been making AYP believed that NCLB was flawed in its foundational assumption of achieving 100 percent proficiency. His seventeen years of experience as a principal plus thirteen as a teacher led him to believe that NCLB was destined to fail:

> The No Child Left Behind Act is one of the most poorly crafted pieces of legislation in the entire history of the U.S. Congress. Forget that it is an unfunded mandate. It attempts to create the impression that it is possible to have one standard for every child or school nationwide. Yet, as we well know, this is not the case.
>
> In fact, there is not even unanimity among the 50 states as to a definition for Adequate Yearly Progress or what standards should be met; leaving both of those up to individual states to decide. But, worst of all, it creates the false impression that *all* students can meet some artificial level of achievement called "proficiency." Those of us in education know this to be patently absurd. A worthy aspiration, but an absolute impossibility. Not *every* child can meet such a level. If that were the case, there would be no 2nd chair clarinet players or students earning D's or F's. What the law fails to take into account is the human and socio-economic factors . . . (aside from measuring a school's worth based upon a one-shot, large-group test score by 3rd or 5th graders) in measuring a student or school's worth.[25]

The principal of a school on one of Minnesota's Native American reservations was more optimistic about the law's intentions but was also very concerned about the academic proficiency targets, particularly in the connection between poverty and proficiency. Despite his worries about his school's prospects for the next year, particularly in light of a student population that made his school one of the poorest in the state, the school made AYP.

The school is a high risk school on an Indian Reservation, with high minority and high poverty. Although we made AYP last year, we will surely soon be a school identified as needing improvement. I have many thoughts on NCLB, but none of them are positive. It's great in theory, but unrealistic in practice to think that schools will achieve 100%. This year, we had a special ed. kid who refused to take the 7th grade . . . reading test. He was one-on-one with two teachers and they could not get him to pick up the pencil and attempt even one answer on the test. With our small numbers, this could put us on "needs improvement" status. Is this any fault of the school or my leadership, I think not. I also am not sure how the school can be responsible for student attendance. Are we supposed to go and drag the kids out of their homes if their parents decide they don't have to come to school? I could go on and on.

Other principals focused on some of the additional problems and uncertainties inherent in NCLB's exclusive focus on the results of one-day snapshots of only one aspect of the truly educated child, including worries about the consequences for the learning of the state's most gifted children:

I'm not sure our high ability students are benefiting because too much time and resources are going to the ones who are failing.

Will kids retain what they've been taught under the stress of test scores and student achievement, AYP, etc.? Or would they be better off making meaning and connections to real life rather than almost a "roteness" to the learning or teaching to the test [way] of educating?

I do not have a teacher (of 55) that is excited about NCLB. We will successfully "dummy-down" our curriculum . . . and ensure we have fewer National Merit scholars, etc.

One of the biggest areas of concern among this small group of Minnesota principals was the failure to address the fundamental issue of resource inequalities between schools and students before trying to hold schools accountable to the challenge of success for all:

> Students are more than numbers. They are unique individuals with thoughts, desires, dreams, talents and imaginations. These do not show up on multiple choice tests! No one wants to leave any child behind. We can provide visionary and effective leadership but the federal government needs to provide our families support for their children by helping to provide an economy where there is "No family left without a job or a home!" We can take it from there.

> I support the idea of standards for student achievement and staff qualifications. I question the idea of putting so much pressure on states to achieve and compete against each other, that AYP is used in a punitive way. I fear that mandates create inequity as poor districts or districts with large numbers of students who have risk factors for low achievement work to overcome those built in obstacles. It takes proportionately larger amounts of resources that are always in short supply.

> Any child who improves his/her skills is a benefit. But if students move to other schools because they perceive that other places achieve better scores, the funds that go with them will also move. That will make it more difficult to keep good staff and fund our system which is successful for many, many students.

Not all of the principals whom I interviewed, however, were pessimistic about No Child Left Behind's prospects. The principal of one school that had achieved five-star status despite its relatively high population of students eligible for free or reduced-price lunch saw NCLB's focus on accountability as beneficial:

> The accountability movement is something I believe in, as I know that many public schools in this country do a poor job of utilizing their resources to meet the needs of students. When I describe some of the things we have implemented at our

school to fellow principals, they look shocked. The model of continuous improvement, which is what I believe is the basic [tenet] of NCLB, has resulted in a positive impact on student achievement.

Others agreed or at least were willing to give No Child Left Behind the benefit of the doubt:

> The actual testing is only a small part of what NCLB is all about. It is about great teaching and smart teaching. All aspects of my leadership go into working with staff to achieve student achievement. I have always believed that in order to lead we need to take an occasional leap of faith. So I actually feel energized by this legislation. My only regret is the lack of funding to [our] school. But without funding it will take a little more time and creative energy. These are challenging times. We can make them [worthwhile] or we can sink with the sinking ship. I personally prefer to face the challenge and make it fun.

> I know that we will work on "test taking." This will mean leaving other areas out of the mix. I believe we will see increase in achievement in some areas and a decrease in achievement in others. I know that we will take a serious look at how we do things. It is always good to reflect on what and why we do what we do. I know positive changes will come of this.

The patterns of cautious optimism about No Child Left Behind's prospects, though often framed within specific concerns, observed in the empirical data could result from either agency concerns (in that these principals feel less powerful in relation to their teachers or other actors and welcome No Child Left Behind's stick) or desperation and frustration (in that something needs to be done, even if it is a flawed strategy). The interview responses suggest that NCLB's good intentions may be hampered by poor design. Support also appears to exist for the beneficial aspects of the law in terms of bureaucratic agency, in that the law—if properly designed—might give principals useful tools for motivating and guiding teachers.

No Child Left Behind and Principals' Influence

To disaggregate the relationship between NCLB's potential effects on influence and a principal's status from the many confounding influences on leadership and achievement, I constructed a series of regression models using the student, school, and principal characteristics discussed in chapter 3. In this case, however, I sought to determine whether being a principal of a regular public school that has achieved AYP status, of a regular public school that has failed, or of a charter school has any systematic relationship to that individual's view of NCLB's leadership consequences.

The key variables are principals' responses to the question, "During the 2003–4 academic year, to what extent will the No Child Left Behind Act limit or enhance your influence on the following policy areas at your school?" The policy areas were (1) setting performance standards, (2) guiding the curriculum, (3) setting discipline policy, (4) hiring and evaluating teachers, and (5) setting the budget. The responses were coded from one (limit very much) to five (enhance very much).

Most Minnesota principals anticipated that No Child Left Behind would enhance their ability to set performance standards in their schools, though nearly a third felt that the law would limit their influence in this area (table A7). In addition, a significant percentage of principals believed that NCLB would facilitate their ability to establish a curriculum. From this perspective, the law might allow principals to push for standards and curricular reform, since they would now be able to argue that the law was forcing these changes. Similarly, smaller but sizable percentages of principals expected that NCLB would make it easier for them to evaluate their teachers, lending some support to the agency view of NCLB's potential utility for those who assume that principals need more carrots with which to entice their teachers.

These data have a few important limitations, and other considerations must be taken into account. First, these analyses are based on self-reports, though the perceptual side of the equation may very well be important in its own right. Second, the 2004 data set lacks a sufficiently large number of charter school principals whose schools failed to make AYP in the previous year. These models present only the probabilities conditional on holding the other indicator variable at zero. In other words, these data do not permit an examination of the specific effects of AYP failure on the charter school principalship beyond its effects on the public school principalship in general, because only four charter schools in the sample had failed to make AYP in 2003. Nevertheless, I believe that much useful information can be gained from the analysis.

Finally, any observed relationship between being a principal in a failing or charter school and that principal's leadership may result from aspects of their leadership and the type of school in which they teach, and this relationship may not be random but may instead be based on unobservable factors. This issue, however, is less of a concern here. The leadership patterns that I observed in chapter 3 showed that principals in schools that were more likely to fail based on the demographic makeup of their student populations spent more, not less, time on the things that translate into higher achievement.

For charter school principals, however, the story is more complicated. Because of their unique nature and greater autonomy, charter schools may attract different kinds of principals. Any observed leadership patterns might result from these inherent differences in the principals rather than in the structure of the charter school principalship itself. In terms of demographic characteristics of principals, some notable differences exist. While only 38 percent of Minnesota's regular public school principals are female, 60 percent of the charter schools in my study were led by women principals. Charter school principals are also less likely to have doctorates and averaged about five years' total experience as a principal versus ten for their regular public school counterparts.

I have, therefore, taken two steps to account for these possible endogeneity effects. The first is to use more complicated statistical techniques to see if my original findings hold up when confronting possible bias.[26] The second step was to include a principal's age, gender, race, and ethnicity in all of the analyses in this chapter.[27] I am somewhat agnostic regarding the question of whether charter school leaders act differently because charter schools attract different types of leaders or because they allow principals to act differently. No doubt, the answer probably includes some of both factors. Unless a state has so many charter schools that the drain of the best principals from the regular public schools becomes an issue (which Minnesota does not), however, we should focus on the possibility that charter schools' advantage may result at least in part from their ability to facilitate a different kind of principalship.

With these considerations in mind, I now turn to the empirical results of my study of the effects of No Child Left Behind on princi-palship in Minnesota, beginning with a more systematic look at how principals expect their influence to change under No Child Left Behind. The underlying regressions suggest a few important results. First, looking at the relationship between charter school status and the mean expected consequences of NCLB shows that charter school principals have much lower expectations about the law's effects on their influence in general (table A9). In contrast, there is no clear indication that principals facing AYP identification generally expect to have more or less influence, possibly either because AYP failure has no impact on principals' expectations or because failure is asso-ciated with expected gains in influence in some areas and loss of influence in others.

Figure 11 presents the predicted percentages of principals who think that NCLB will enhance their influence across the six school policy areas, broken down by whether the principal's school is a reg-ular public school that made AYP, a regular school that failed to do so, or a charter school. Again, these analyses separate the relation-ships among NCLB, charter schools, and leadership from all of the other possibly correlated factors, especially student and school char-acteristics.

Of all of the areas of leadership about which they were asked, only in setting performance standards did a majority of principals feel that No Child Left Behind would enhance their influence. This finding indicates that top-down accountability might be useful if it provides principals with the tools to guide their schools to higher levels of per-formance. In addition, principals of traditional public schools that failed to make AYP were more optimistic about their ability to set per-formance standards and evaluate their teachers than those whose

Predicted Percentages of Principals Reporting That NCLB
Will Enhance Their Influence

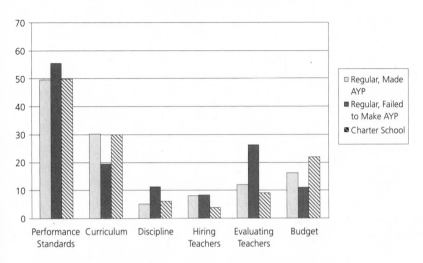

Question:

"During the 2003–2004 academic year, to what extent will the No Child Left Behind Act limit or enhance your influence on the following policy areas at your school?" Coded 1 = "Limit very much," 2 = "Limit somewhat," 3 = "No effect," 4 = "Enhance somewhat," 5 = "Enhance very much."

Fig. 11. Expected consequences of NCLB on principal's influence. (Probabilities obtained using Clarify [see King, Tomz, and Wittenberg 2000]. *Source:* Minnesota Schools Survey 2003. Demographic and AYP data from Minnesota Department of Education 2003c, 2003d, 2004a.)

schools made AYP according to the lists published three months earlier but were less optimistic about their ability to establish the curriculum and spend the school's budget. Principals in schools that failed to make AYP were more than twice as likely as either of the other groups to report that No Child Left Behind would enhance their influence in evaluating their teachers.

These findings lend more support to the idea that at least some of the perceived benefits of No Child Left Behind are explained by the agency view of the principalship. NCLB involves a trade-off of influence, but principals might be willing to make this deal if they believe that it will allow them to get closer to their goal of improving academic achievement. The threat of sanction can be beneficial if strategically used, a logic similar to that of the president drawing a hard line with a foreign power and claiming that an intransigent Congress has tied his hands.

Charter school principals generally displayed patterns of expected influence that closely resembled those of their counter-parts in traditional public schools that made AYP. The principals of charter schools were, however, more skeptical than their colleagues at regular public schools about NCLB's likely effects on their influence in hiring and evaluating teachers, a finding that is not sur-prising given the greater autonomy that charter school principals enjoy in these areas (although it is not possible to rule out the possi-bility that these differences in expectations result from chance). That charter school principals felt more optimistic about NCLB's effects on their budget-setting abilities is surprising, though the underlying coefficient estimates are not significant. Further study of this finding might be warranted.

While expected consequences are interesting, it is more instruc-tive to compare patterns of influence among principals whose schools have made or failed to make AYP. Observers have extensively discussed whether teachers teach to the tests but have given much less thought to the question of whether principals lead to the tests and to whether this would be a desirable outcome. The next set of simulations is based on a set of regression models that examines prin-cipals' perceptions of their influence in these six school policy areas. In the Minnesota survey, principals were asked to respond to the question, "How much actual influence do you think you as principal have regarding the following policy areas at your school?" for six school policy areas: setting performance standards, establishing the curriculum, hiring teachers, evaluating teachers, setting discipline policy, and spending the budget. While the basic regression models underlying these simulations resembled those in figure 11, these models also included principals' views on the influence of parents, teachers, and the Minnesota Department of Education as a means of capturing the fact that principals are embedded in a complex web of agency relationships that affect the exercise of the others' power.[28]

Some clear patterns emerge from the underlying regressions. In contrast to predictions that principal and teacher power exist in opposition to each other—a view that most scholars of agency in educational production have asserted—principals in my study felt that their influence was positively tied to that of their teachers across all six of the school policy areas examined (table A10). All of these relationships were statistically significant. The notion of educational production as a zero-sum administrative game in which principals are constantly at war with their teachers is much too simplistic in the framework of experiential organizations, where school principals try to assemble the best team that they can and lead by fighting with and for their teachers. This of course does not mean that no conflict arises, only that principals are most effective when they do not have to constantly monitor their teachers.

Interestingly, principals felt that their influence was positively tied to the influence of parents and of the Minnesota Department of Education, but only in those areas where one actor's contributions might offset the power of another. The principals in my study felt that their influence was positively related to that of their parents when setting performance standards and guiding the curriculum and was positively related to that of the Minnesota Department of Education in enforcing discipline policy and to a lesser extent in setting performance standards and hiring teachers.

The simulation results derived from a look at principals' views of their influence challenge the most optimistic expectations of the bureaucratic consequences of No Child Left Behind, both on the part of policymakers and on the part of the principals (figure 12). AYP failure (announced during the summer) is associated with lower levels of influence across all six areas of school policy during the following fall. These differences were statistically significant in two critical areas: setting performance standards and guiding the development of the curriculum.[29] Principals of schools that have failed to make AYP were 63 percent less likely to report that they had a great deal of influence in setting performance standards in the school and 59 percent less likely to report that they had a great deal of influence in guiding the curriculum within the school.

The two areas where Minnesota's principals expected the greatest

Predicted Percentages of Principals Reporting a Great Deal of Influence

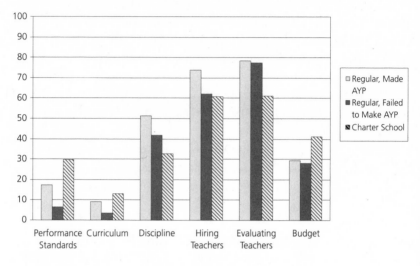

Question:

"How much <u>actual influence</u> do you think you <u>as principal</u> have regarding the following <u>policy areas at your school</u>?" Coded: from 1 = "No influence" to 5 = "A great deal of influence."

Fig. 12. Influence of principal in policy areas. (Probabilities obtained using Clarify [see King, Tomz, and Wittenberg 2000]. *Source:* Minnesota Schools Survey 2003. Demographic and AYP data from Minnesota Department of Education 2003c, 2003d, 2004a.)

benefit from No Child Left Behind in the previous analysis—setting performance standards and establishing the curriculum—were also the two areas where they felt the least influential. The two areas where they felt the most influential—hiring and evaluating teachers—were also two of the three areas where they perceived the least benefit from NCLB.

These patterns are entirely consistent with what James Q. Wilson predicted about top-down reforms in coping organizations. Of course, one might counter that we want these principals in failing schools to be less influential since whatever they were doing was not working. This conclusion, however, rests on the assumption that AYP failure results only from leadership, not from things beyond the control of principals and teachers, which I have established is not the case. This assertion also rests on the assumption that the law bases its confiscation of principal autonomy on a true measure of the quality of the principal's efforts in developing and implementing the school's curriculum.

Charter school principals, in contrast, perceive themselves as less influential in setting discipline policy (possibly as a consequence of greater influence by their customers) and hiring and evaluating their teachers but more influential in setting performance standards, guiding the curriculum, and spending the budget. These patterns are consistent with the expected findings, given these principals' greater autonomy in these areas. The differences for charter schools are statistically significant in setting performance standards and discipline policy as well as in evaluating teachers.

NCLB and the Influence of Other Actors in Education

Principals are only one of many sets of actors in education, and it is useful to relate what they think about the influence of these players in the educational policy space to the top-down and bottom-up reforms in place. Figure 13 breaks down the predicted percentages of principals who feel that each of four actors in the educational policy space has a great deal of influence in making decisions that affect their schools by the same status variables as before: whether the principal is leading a school that made AYP, whether she is leading a failing school, or whether she is the principal of a charter school. This set of models, similar in all other ways to those in figure 12, examines principals' responses to the question, "How much actual influence do you think each of the following has regarding making decisions that affect your school?" for four actors in the educational policy space: principals, teachers, parents, and the Minnesota Department of Education. Both of these sets of responses were coded on a five-point scale, where zero equals no influence and five equals a great deal of influence.[30]

Minnesota's public school principals were much more likely to report that officials with the Department of Education had a great

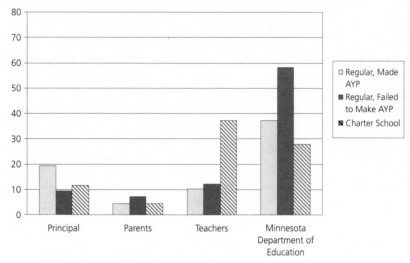

Question:
"How much actual influence do you think each of the following has regarding making decisions that affect your school?" Coded: from 1 = "No influence" to 5 = "A great deal of influence."

Fig. 13. Influence of actors in education. (Probabilities obtained using Clarify [see King, Tomz, and Wittenberg 2000]. *Source:* Minnesota Schools Survey 2003. Demographic and AYP data from Minnesota Department of Education 2003c, 2003d, 2004a.)

deal of influence than any of the other three sets of actors and were much less likely to report that parents had a great deal of influence in their schools. This pattern echoes a long-standing criticism of public education in the United States: that the inevitable product of democratic control over education results in the ossification of control over schooling and undue influence by bureaucrats far removed from the actual production of education.[31]

Some notable differences in influence also exist among these groups of principals. Charter school principals were more than three times as likely to report that their teachers had a great deal of influence than either group of regular public school principals and the least likely of the three groups to report that the Minnesota Department of Education had a great deal of influence.[32] Principals in regular public schools that failed to make AYP, however, were more than 50 percent more likely than those whose schools made AYP to report that the Minnesota Department of Education had a great deal of influence in setting policy in their schools. These principals, however, were less than half as likely to perceive themselves as very influential than their counterparts in schools that had not been so labeled. As noted in chapter 3, these results cannot prove that AYP sanction causes the Minnesota Department of Education to become more powerful and principals less powerful. However, these correlations are entirely consistent with such an explanation and concur with my theoretical predictions. If one believes that AYP identification is based on a true measure of the quality of the principalship and that the answer to this failure is to increase the power of state officials, then No Child Left Behind appears to be a bureaucratic success. Both of these assumptions are questionable at best and misguided at worst.

These patterns of influence are entirely consistent with the predictions of chapter 2 (and those made by Wilson) about the contrast between top-down and bottom-up reforms. If policymakers evaluate schools from the top down, they end up increasing their influence and decreasing that of those closer to educational production. If, however, policymakers pass the ultimate evaluations of quality to the consumers of the services, they increase the power of those close to the real action and decrease the power of those farther away from it.

The complex relationships among expectations, influence, and agency observed in the survey results were echoed in the open-ended comments that principals provided in the follow-up interviews. Those principals who were optimistic about NCLB's potential consequences for Minnesota's public schools tended to locate the benefits within the agency relationships in which the schools are embedded because such relationships give the principals either additional tools for evaluating their leadership or additional levers with which to bring along teachers and staff. For the principal of a five-star school, the benefits of No Child Left Behind derived from having more information with which to assess his school's progress toward his goals. Though potentially at a disadvantage given his school's high proportion of students eligible for free or reduced-price lunch, he welcomed the focus on students in all subgroups:

> From my perspective NCLB has been a driving force behind several positive changes in my school. Our desire as a staff is to do our best for kids, and I have been able to use the NCLB legislation to promote the need to work smarter and focus more on moving all students forward academically. I believe that my teachers have always strived to do their best, and NCLB is just one more program that is assisting us in defining what we do on a daily basis.
>
> I am very concerned with the rhetoric I hear from many of my principal colleagues regarding NCLB. They view this as a Bush mandate, and therefore it is all bad. My approach has been to focus on the positives of the legislation, including the training of paraprofessionals, using research based curriculum, measuring student growth from year to year, and addressing the various subgroups that need a more specialized approach to helping them catch up. I believe that my leadership and how I have responded to NCLB has actually improved the working conditions for teachers. We have developed better systems to help students, monitor achievement, etc. which has resulted in a smarter working environment.

An elementary school principal in another part of the state framed the benefits of No Child Left Behind directly in terms of agency relationships. With twenty-four years of teaching under her belt, she welcomed the chance to encourage her staff to do more:

> My leadership has been affected positively by NCLB. The staff at this school are very resistant to change. The changes that have been needed can be moved forward better because we have a goal and expectation. I speak of NCLB as a goal that is good, and it can help us focus what we do. My philosophy is that if we are addressing the needs of students and focusing

our energy, then communicating this to students and parents and are able to give specific information about how students are doing in relation to the goal each year, we will get more involvement from parents and more motivation from students.

A high school principal with an equally long record of teaching agreed:

NCLB encourages accountability and focus in a district. I believe very much that educators need to be held more accountable for student learning. In this light, my leadership is reinforced by NCLB. I would guess that roughly 20% of my time now is spent trying to insure our school makes AYP. Much of the increase is due to testing, increased demands for documentation, and developing and implementing changes in policies and procedures. I now have less time for other duties, like teacher observation and associated staff development.

As his comments reveal, however, the added focus on excellence and the added ability to motivate and encourage teachers and students do not come without cost. Refocusing efforts invariably means time taken away from other tasks, and having a bigger stick with which to motivate teachers has the very real potential to erode the consensus-building aspects of the public school principalship, a comment echoed by several of his colleagues:

NCLB is just one small aspect of my leadership. However, it has challenged me to move mountains in short order. It has challenged me to become an expert in best practices in curriculum and instruction. It has challenged me to provide learning opportunities for all staff to increase student achievement. These challenges are very exciting; . . . however, they are also very time consuming and draining. . . . The day-to-day operations, being in the hallways with kids, etc., suffer.

I've been more directive—top-down decisions, even though I have a site team. The pressure is on me from my superintendent to produce higher achievement too. It trickles down to teachers and students and parents. I feel that it puts me in a position to "enforce" rather than "support" good teaching. The mandate of NCLB has become a "do it or I'll hurt you" model. . . . [M]ake the progress or you'll end up on the dreaded list.

The principal of one Minnesota's charter schools agreed. With a student population nearly 100 percent nonwhite, a student population eligible for free or reduced-price lunch nearly as high, and having made AYP the year before, the principal felt that No Child Left Behind must be carefully examined for its effects on the broader community that she believes defines what a school is supposed to be about:

If we are to embrace the beliefs of intrinsic motivation and that success is its own reward for our students, we should then set an example of a balanced life, strong work ethic and [acknowledgment] of differences. Too much focus on external rewards turns even the best people into poor citizens. [NCLB's] approach can have some benefits but must be examined very carefully.

Another Minnesota principal perceived it to be part of his job to actively shield his teachers from the stresses and consequences of No Child Left Behind. In terms of bureaucratic agency, he thus sabotages the law's intent. With seventeen years of experience as a principal plus thirteen as a teacher, he felt, however, that part of his professionalism was to act as a counterweight to the power of the Minnesota Department of Education, which his survey responses indicated he believed surpassed that of any of the other actors in the state's educational environment:

As principal, I have made it a point to downplay the importance of the results of tests to my students, staff, and parents. I simply tell the teachers to follow our curriculum scope and sequence and not teach to the test or set aside special test prep times. We encourage our students to be here and do their best; and we encourage the parents to make sure their children are here so we don't get "dunced" for the simple lack of test takers. By putting a priority on good teaching practices, supporting staff development activities to improve those practices, and making school a positive, nurturing environment for students and staff, we hope to create an atmosphere where students are able to do their best . . . no matter what that "best" is.

When reflecting on the effects of NCLB on the influence of their teachers, the small group of Minnesota's principals in my follow-up interviews worried about the reallocation of teachers' time and energy and the prospect of risk aversion in their approach to their jobs. Mostly, however, they focused on the stress that the law causes their teachers, a group without which—as the survey results show—principals do not feel that they can effectively do their jobs.

We have wonderful teachers. They work hard and do a great job of meeting needs. My concern is the extra, unnecessary pressure added to them due to NCLB. They work hard and care. . . . [T]hey should be given credit for that.

My teachers are very stressed out. While we have taken great steps to provide them with a positive attitude and excellent staff development and resources to support students and learning, teachers typically don't move this quickly. This has been a very overwhelming year for many. Also, recognizing that they have to teach all children with the expectation that they all perform at or above grade level is a new concept for the middle schools.

They are stressed. . . . [T]est scores drive teaching now, more than ever, and [NCLB is] increasing the amount of pressure for teachers and principals.

Many principals also felt that the added stress placed on teachers would lead not to increased academic achievement but to risk aversion and a narrowing of the curriculum, just as the theoretical framework in chapter 2 predicts:

The teachers prepare for the tests. They are accountable for test scores. This makes the teachers more irritable and less willing to try new things in class.

Teachers are more nervous about how students do on tests and spend more time on test related items and less on creative mind expanding activities. They have less time to help develop the total student emotionally, physically, and academically. [The] staff has been less inclined to look at new and different things. I encourage their taking risks but not as many are willing or have the time to try new things at this point.

When our school scores are being measured against the other scores of schools around us, I believe people feel they need to concentrate on the things that are measured. In some ways this is good, but it has decreased the willingness on teachers' parts to try to [do] new things or approaches.

Teachers are spending less time on social skills, art, music, science, academic survival skills, and social studies and more time on math and reading. Teachers are spending less time on gifted and talented students, the best readers and mathematicians.

A few principals saw the stress of NCLB's potential consequences as forcing a change in the character of the principalship itself, as they found themselves engaged in activities that they had not imagined as traditional roles, such as providing damage control and protection for their students and staff:

Last year one of the elementary buildings was identified early on as a school [in need of] improvement. Later it was determined that it was a clerical error which had placed the school on the list. Even in this situation the hours of time that it required to deal with this situation was a tremendous amount of lost resources and very little educational value. I had conducted numerous interviews with the media over this period of time as well as drafting responses to the school board, community, and state department.

I have staff members who tell me that NCLB has taken the fun out of teaching and learning. Kids can't just be kids anymore. Teachers in grades 3 and 5 feel added stress. There is so much to teach and not enough time to do it. I know I am not alone in my beliefs, many elementary principals are just too nice (or diplomatic) to say it.

The challenge to my leadership is to protect the staff from the outside impacting agencies and policies and to allow them the freedom to engage their students to become the citizens for future generations of leaders.

These responses raise a critical concern, again brought up in the theoretical discussions of chapter 2: that No Child Left Behind's peculiar method of top-down accountability may lead to an ultimately counterproductive reallocation of principals' limited time and energy toward fulfilling the narrow vision of educational quality embodied in the law's one-size-fits-all approach to identification and sanction.

NCLB and Principals' Allocation of Time

This chapter's final analysis involves a closer empirical look at how No Child Left Behind affects how principals spend their time, which is probably their scarcest and easily their most valuable asset. Figure 14 presents the relationship between status as a target of AYP identification, status as an example of bottom-up charter school reforms, and the way in which principals allocate their time.[33] One of the foundational assumptions of this analysis is that principals allocate this scarce resource as best they can in response to the continually arising demands on their energy and efforts. As figure 14 shows, principals in all three groups were much more likely to have spent a great deal of time on administrative activities than any of the other policy areas about which they were asked. That charter school principals spent a great deal of time on administration is not surprising, given the enormous challenges of finding a home for, organizing, and leading a brand-new school, but it does cast a bit of doubt on the most optimistic claims that charter school principals will be free of all

Predicted Percentages of Principals Reporting a Great Deal of Time Spent

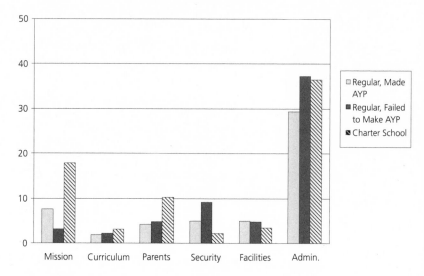

Question:

"During the past month, about how much of your time was spent on the following activities?" Coded: 1 = "None or almost none," 2 = "Slightly less time than on other activities," 3 = "About as much time as other activities," 4 = "Slightly more time than other activities," 5 = "A great deal of time."

Fig. 14. Principals' allocation of time. (Probabilities obtained using Clarify [see King, Tomz, and Wittenberg 2000]. *Source:* Minnesota Schools Survey 2003. Demographic and AYP data from Minnesota Department of Education 2003c, 2003d, 2004a.)

administrative duties to focus on parents and curriculum. This question will be more easily addressed when there are large numbers of charter schools that have existed for longer periods of time.

The results show that charter school principals differed substantially from their counterparts in traditional public schools in spending much more time facilitating their school's mission and reaching out to their parent communities. Both of these differences are statistically significant and are consonant with what the effective schools researchers called good leadership. Charter school principals also spent less time supervising their faculty, a difference that was statistically significant. The probabilities that either group would spend a great deal of time on this activity, however, were so small that I did not include it in figure 14. Wilson suggests that coping organizations will be characterized by adversarial manager-operator relationships: charter school principals may supervise their faculty less because they feel that they can do so.

With principals in regular public schools that failed to make AYP, the important story is partly what we see but mostly what we do not see. Failure is not associated with a corresponding rededication to those aspects of the principalship that increase test scores and decrease the probability of future failure and sanction under No Child Left Behind. Principals in regular public schools that failed to make AYP are less focused on the school mission than those not identified, a statistically significant difference. Neither the variable for having failed to make AYP nor the variable indicating status as principal of charter school were significant in a regression on the mean amount of time spent on all activities, indicating that differences really exist in the patterns of time allocation; the findings do not show merely that principals feel more overwhelmed by the demands of their jobs because of AYP failure or by the stresses associated with starting and operating a charter school.

Even the principals who expressed support for No Child Left Behind in the follow-up interviews generally agreed that the law led to a reallocation of their time and energy toward meeting the law's requirements and away from other, perhaps more fundamental, aspects of their leadership. Again, such a change could be beneficial, if the law is measuring true quality. Given the finite nature of the resource, some of this reallocation of time came at the expense of other leadership areas, and while some came from the principals' personal lives. The principal of a metro-area middle school that failed to make AYP found the demands overwhelming:

> NCLB has had a direct impact on my leadership at school. I spend significant time out of the building, working with district office personnel, understanding all the ramifications, interventions, data, etc. . . . I also spend 12–14 hour days. . . . [I]t is after 5:00 P.M. even as I write and I will be here for at least a 12

hour day. . . . [T]here is much to do with little support. I spend a significant amount of time ensuring that my school is making AYP. . . . I realize that in principle this is a wonderful thing . . . every child at grade level. However, I need a partner to take on some of the "regular" principal business while I take this on.

Others—even those who favored the law—concurred with the sense of increased demands:

I am all for school improvement, using research based methodology, and analyzing test data. Schools are not factories. When I hear the phrase "No Child Left Behind," my staff and I cringe. For those of us from Minnesota, NCLB is a step backwards. We spend way too much time testing, doing paperwork, and trying to figure out what we are suppose[d] to do. It has created more work for secretaries, business managers, paraprofessionals, teachers, and administrators. I'm talking hours.

I spend more time with data and accountability, yet have to pull from my family to do it. The only way to keep up is to work longer and longer. If this would lead to higher achievement, it may be worthwhile. However, we need to have time working with the instructional aspects, too. We simply don't have time to hold teachers accountable for instruction.

Many of the things I already did as we have always strived to be a high performing school and embrace educational reform. I would estimate that exploring data takes at least extra 5 days each year. Testing takes about 10 days out of my year. Staff development issues consume another 3 days. [The] service time I spend and additional time writing the district Title grant add another 10 days. Add additional state reports all in one way or another tying into AYP it adds about 30 days time in total taken away from other duties I used to perform. Some do not get done, some are shortchanged, and some I do by adding on to my day or year.

I am much more in tune with data about school performance.

I spend a lot of time sharing information about standards with my staff and curriculum groups. It seems that I am always looking for explanations for what I consider or others could consider low performance, but trying not to use excuses. Public relations is a big deal.

The first thing the students hear on the radio and television on testing days is "how are the students in your child's school measuring up?" This year on one of the testing days I was bombarded 5 times from the media about the day's testing and how well our school was doing before I got to school, and I live across the street from building. Now we have school report cards handed out at the state fair!

Time is a finite and scarce commodity. If we can be sure that a high-stakes testing policy is forcing this reallocation on the basis of accurate measures of the quality of educational production, then we can be more optimistic. As I have shown, however, this is a highly doubtful proposition.

Conclusions

Nothing in these analyses suggests that No Child Left Behind cannot work, only that given its current assessment regime, it does not yet appear to be producing the kinds of positive leadership responses that it is designed to create. Principals in traditional public schools that are not making AYP present very different patterns of leadership and influence than their nonidentified counterparts, patterns that suggest effects on leadership that will make it less rather than more likely for principals in identified schools to improve their performance. Of course, these findings do not mean that innovative schools are doomed to fail under NCLB—good leaders will always try to find ways to lead—only that the incentives structures currently in place run counter to the goal of educational innovation.[34]

Principals in charter schools, also subject to the quality assessments of their parent communities, appear to be more focused on those aspects of leadership that the effective schools literature has shown to be associated with producing better quality in education. I have not been able to comment on the charter-school-specific leadership consequences of No Child Left Behind. NCLB may produce a different, better bureaucratic response in charter schools than appears to be the case in traditional public schools. The data from Minnesota are not sufficient to refute this possibility. Given the high probability of sanction for charter schools, however, NCLB would need to induce or reinforce in charter school principals enough of an increase in customer, curricular, and mission orientation to overcome the destructive implications of sanction—an unlikely prospect. Either time-series studies or well-chosen microlevel work will be needed to confirm or refute the findings of these preliminary studies.

There is nothing inherently incompatible with top-down and bottom-up reforms in education; however, NCLB's current requirements do not properly align incentives and behaviors in the best way possible. If being accountable to parents and having bureaucratic autonomy are beneficial, then there is no reason to withhold these benefits from the regular public schools and give them only to the charter schools. This is where NCLB, properly conceived and executed, could be a powerful and positive force in educational reform. If we can incorporate assessments that motivate traditional public school principals to listen to their parent communities and if we can design incentives to reward these principals for excellence with autonomy as well as resources, then we have the chance of making a system that not only is top-down and bottom-up driven but also self-reinforcing rather than self-contradictory.

Charter schools represent only one means of creating a more autonomous and responsive principalship, and they may not even be the most promising way given the extraordinary challenges inherent in creating a new set of financially sound, stable, and excellent schools. As part of a state's implementation of NCLB, a system could be created to identify outstanding public school principals, to better align their interests with those of their customers, and to provide them with the support needed to fulfill the critical ambitions of No Child Left Behind.

CHAPTER 5

Rethinking Assessment

Ask the teachers, ask the kids, ask the parents,
and look at test scores and other measures of
success. One single test score can't possibly tell
the story of leadership.

Minnesota school principal, in response to a
question about how to measure his leadership

The results of the analyses in the previous chapters provide cause for
concern but also for hope. Unfortunately, identification under No
Child Left Behind appears to be related mostly to factors that principals and teachers cannot control. Identification also appears to produce the kinds of unfortunate bureaucratic responses that the theory
predicts. NCLB is also making survival of large numbers of diverse
public, alternative, and charter schools unlikely, particularly as we
approach the later stages of its implementation. This large-scale failure remains highly likely even though the principals of many of these
schools are doing the types of things that lead to higher-quality education. However, the underlying endeavor does not appear to be
futile. Principals' leadership can have a positive effect on academic
achievement, leaving open the possibility that a top-down accountability system that rewarded good leadership could lead to closing
the achievement gap between minority and nonminority, advantaged

and disadvantaged students. This finding, combined with the fact that top-down accountability appears, for better or worse, to constrain and control principals' ability to lead and organize their schools, leaves open the possibility that No Child Left Behind can work if we get the assessments and the incentives right. In this chapter, I ask:

> If we wish to preserve the goals and achieve the promised benefits of top-down accountability, how can we do a better job?

Central to this prospect would be a measurement system that allowed policymakers to draw meaningful quality distinctions between schools that serve disadvantaged student populations without universally condemning them to identification and sanction. In this chapter, I consider three alternative approaches to identifying educational quality under a top-down system such as No Child Left Behind. Researchers and policymakers have already discussed the first two approaches but not the third. They represent increasingly significant modifications to NCLB's testing regimen. Briefly, they involve evaluating schools based on

> the yearly change in the percentages of students achieving state standards;
> the change in proficiency of a given student in a given year; and
> the conditions of production within the schools.

Though the specific provisions of evaluation systems may seem a bit esoteric and detailed, their effects are hardly inconsequential.

Growth Models of Assessment

The failings of the current approach of evaluating schools based only on the percentages of their students that meet a state set standard are now familiar. These systems do a very good job of singling out schools with high-minority, low-income student populations. These kinds of systems are sometimes called "status models," as they provide only a snapshot of student performance at a given point in time and "cannot factor out year-to-year changes in student body composition or grade-to-grade changes in instructional design or teacher quality."[1] Perhaps, some observers have argued, status models are useful for descriptive purposes and for identifying schools with underperforming students so that more resources can be sent their way.[2] This, however, is not what No Child Left Behind was designed to do.

In contrast, several researchers and policymakers have proposed that we evaluate students based on changes in overall academic achievement from year to year. These are often called "gain" or "growth" models, because they reflect gains in proficiency rather than overall levels of proficiency.[3] In theory, their application is straightforward. One simply analyzes the year-by-year changes in the percentages of students—overall and, if desired, among racial, ethnic, or other subgroups of students—that meet the relevant proficiency targets.

The logic behind growth models makes intuitive sense. Schools that are coasting on the laurels of their already well-educated students will not automatically be identified as outstanding, though their high levels of proficiency would likely shield these schools from sanction in a regime that combined growth models with the status models currently in use; however, schools that took their student populations from very low levels of proficiency to significantly higher levels would be rewarded rather than punished for their performance, even if their schools still scored below a state's proficiency requirements.

Growth models present several issues, however. Perhaps the biggest challenge is the problem of regression to the mean, whereby outstanding gains in one year are likely to be followed by less spectacular results in the following year, not because of anything that is happening in the schools but because these numbers bounce around a lot and randomness and noise are inherent in any system: "A large portion of the change in test scores from one year to the next could be the result of sampling variation and other nonpersistent causes."[4] Regression to the mean is why investing in last year's hot mutual fund is usually a bad idea. In testing, like finance, past performance may not always be a good indicator of future performance.

Other problems arise as well. Any growth model must account for the fact that given student mobility, especially in low-income areas, the group of students that takes the tests in one year will not be the same as the group tested in another year. The systemic consequences are also potentially significant. Schools that take in large numbers of lower-performing students in one year would be penalized for doing so, since the new population would be compared to a very different cohort of students. This is an issue of fairness, for sure, but it is also an issue of incentives. School administrators might be much less likely to open their doors to lower-achieving students under a public choice system if they felt that they might be penalized for doing so (although the status models currently in use also provide incentives not to reach out to lower-performing students). One researcher has commented on the political challenges likely to arise with the widespread use of gain-score models: "The public is unlikely to soon consider a school progressing from the 5th to the 10th percentile as more successful than a school declining from the 95th to the 90th percentile."[5] Finally, it is not at all clear that a lifetime of resource inequalities is less relevant to gains in academic achievement than to measured achievement in one year. Poverty's half-life may not be so short as this.

In response to some of these concerns, other variants of growth models have been proposed. One would be to track the achievement of specific cohorts of students as they progress through the schools. This "cohort gain model,"[6] while arguably providing a more accurate reflection of the experiences of specific groups of students, still suffers from some of the same problems of any gain model of assessment: student mobility and the possibility that resource differences might affect growth in achievement just as much as absolute achievement.

In November 2005, U.S. Secretary of Education Margaret Spellings announced a national program designed to encourage and allow ten state pilot programs using growth models to measure adequate yearly progress (AYP): "A growth model is not a way around accountability standards. It's a way for states that are already raising achievement and following the bright-line principles of the law to strengthen accountability."[7] While acknowledging the move to be a step in the right direction, the president of the National Education

Association quickly criticized Spellings's plan as insufficient: "Unfortunately, the Department's move does not go far enough because students in a maximum of 10 states will be able to benefit from this more reasonable and valid growth model, leaving students in classrooms in the rest of the country with the very same model the Department has identified as flawed."[8]

Several states had already begun to experiment with growth models of measurement prior to NCLB's passage or during the early years of its implementation. Florida's A+ system, for example, scores schools on a point system that involves both percentages of students meeting state standards and gains in student achievement within schools. If Florida's experience is to be a guide, then state and national policymakers should prepare for some confusion when the pilot programs attempt to fuse static and growth models within the same accountability system. As a Florida Parent-Teacher Association president remarked, "'I think there is a real lack of understanding about how these school grades are put together.'"[9]

Given these potential benefits and limitations, it seems worthwhile to begin to explore what might happen if Minnesota adopted a growth model to see if those schools identified as performing or underperforming would differ from the patterns that emerge under the current status model of assessment. Table 5 presents summary data for the 5 percent of Minnesota's public and charter schools that made the greatest gains in the percentages of their students meeting proficiency targets for the third-grade reading tests between 2003 and 2004. Table 6 presents the same summary data for the top 5 percent of gainers on the third-grade mathematics tests.[10]

Minnesota's top gaining schools in grade three reading and mathematics scores made significant progress in the percentages of students meeting the state's proficiency targets. Though, as one would expect, the top-gaining schools started from much lower levels of success—less than half of the students in these schools met reading and math proficiency targets in 2003—they increased the proficiency rate by more than 50 percent in both subjects. These top-gaining schools, however, were only more likely to make AYP based on mathematics test scores. The AYP success rates were nearly the same for the top gainers in reading as they were for the rest of the state's ele-

TABLE 5. Minnesota's Top Gainers in Reading, 2003–4

	Top 5% by Grade Three Reading Gain (1)	All Other Schools (2)
Average 2003–4 change in percentage of students meeting standards	+24%	–1%
Average 2003 baseline of percentage of students meeting standards	47%	73%
Percentage failing to make AYP in 2004	14%	13%
Percentage of these schools that are charter schools	12%	3%
Percentage of students who are . . .		
Of minority race and/or ethnicity	42%	22%
Eligible for free or reduced-price lunch	47%	27%
In special education	14%	13%
LEP	14%	8%
Number of schools	42	792

Source: Author's analysis based on data from Minnesota Department of Education 2003c, 2003d, 2003f, 2004a, 2004d.

TABLE 6. Minnesota's Top Gainers in Math, 2003–4

	Top 5% by Grade Three Math Gain (1)	All Other Schools (2)
Average 2003–4 change in percentage of students meeting standards	+26%	–3%
Average 2003 baseline of percentage of students meeting standards	47%	72%
Percentage failing to make AYP in 2004	7%	14%
Percentage of these schools that are charter schools	14%	3%
Percentage of students who are . . .		
Of minority race and/or ethnicity	34%	22%
Eligible for free or reduced-price lunch	40%	27%
In special education	13%	8%
LEP	9%	9%
Number of schools	42	792

Source: Author's analysis based on data from Minnesota Department of Education 2003c, 2003d, 2003f, 2004a, 2004d.

mentary schools, probably because although these schools made safe harbor overall, they failed to do so for a particular subgroup category, which raises an important concern. Any growth model that focuses only on overall changes runs the risk of leaving subgroups behind if the model does not account for growth in proficiency among all subgroups.

Minnesota's charter schools do much better under this simulated growth model than they do under the state's current status model. While charter schools make up only 3 percent of schools in the state that offer grade three education, they constitute 12 percent (for reading) and 14 percent (for math) of the top gaining schools in these data. The biggest gainers in reading and math are also schools that serve higher-need student populations. Minnesota's best in these simulations have nearly twice the proportions of minority and low-income students.

Growth models also appear to identify public school principals who allocate more of their time to developing the school's mission and guiding development of the curriculum and less time supervising faculty and focusing on facilities and security (table 7). This, of

TABLE 7. Leadership Patterns of Minnesota's Top Gainers in Reading and Math between 2003 and 2004

	Grade 3 Reading (1)	Grade 3 Mathematics (2)
Difference between top 5% of schools and all others in percentage of total time spent on . . .		
Facilitating achievement of the school's mission	+2%	+3%
Supervising faculty	–10%	–4%
Guiding development of the curriculum	+26%	+15%
Building relationships with the parent community	–11%	+4%
Maintaining the physical security of students and staff	–18%	–4%
Managing facilities	–19%	–10%
Completing administrative tasks	+12%	–2%

Source: Minnesota Schools Survey 2003. Test score data from Minnesota Department of Education 2003f, 2004d.

Note: The survey question was worded as follows: "During the past month, about how much of *your time* was spent on the following activities?" Each variable is coded as 1 "None or almost none," 2 "Slightly less time than on other activities," 3 "About as much time as other activities," 4 "Slightly more time than other activities," 5 "A great deal of time."

course, does not necessarily mean that these environments are less clean and safe but only that the principals probably spend less time putting out physical or social fires in spite of the fact that they tend to serve higher-need student populations.

Incorporating any variant of a growth model into No Child Left Behind's system of assessment is of course much more complicated than simply saying it should be done. Doing so involves detailed questions about actual targets and theoretical questions about building in the proper system of incentives. A particular challenge is the use of growth models when analyzing the achievement of specific subgroups. Problems of noise and variation are only compounded when one is looking at test score changes in groups of as few as twenty students, where "a dog barking in the playground on the day of the test, a severe flu season, one particularly disruptive student in a class, or favorable chemistry between a group of students and their teacher"[11] can have a significant impact on measured gains. I will take up these issues in more detail in the final chapter. For now, however, it is useful to note that, based on the small analysis here, growth models have the potential to identify schools that are doing well, especially in resource-poor communities. Any system that incorporated these models would likely not come down as hard on urban and rural public schools or charter schools as the current status models do.

Value-Added Assessment

In contrast to growth models of quality measurement, value-added assessment (VAA) systems seek to analyze educational quality in the way that the term describes—by extracting what value a school or teacher is adding to total achievement of the student in a way that accounts for all of the correlates to success or failure that I have been discussing.[12] In practice, VAA does not differ substantially from my analyses in this book, although of course I have used aggregate rather than student-level data. The similarity lies in the fact that value-added analysis uses regression techniques on a database of individual student test scores over time to account for the myriad of factors that predict academic achievement.

VAA models have gained a considerable amount of support, espe-

cially from those researchers who have focused on the methodological side of implementing No Child Left Behind's mandates. Unlike
status models, which capture schools that serve disproportionately
high numbers of disadvantaged students, VAA measures "can be
designed to eliminate the effects of mobility, affluence, and other
extrinsic factors"[13] from evaluations of school quality.

Like growth models, value-added models of quality assessment
have been and continue to be part of the debate about making NCLB
work in several states. Researchers employing a "massive, longitudi-
nally merged database"[14] of Tennessee student test scores and demographic characteristics along with teacher, school, and district characteristics argued that their analyses extracted a truer measure of
teacher quality than could be attained under simple status models of
quality assessment. The best schools with lower aggregate test scores
actually did better on these measures than schools with higher levels
of total proficiency, a finding that confirmed a 2002 study of the
effectiveness of value-added measures in the Milwaukee public
schools.[15] Neither the Tennessee study nor the Milwaukee study,
however, examined the relationship between the implementation of
value-added analysis and the responses and perceptions of principals
and teachers. Interestingly, the author of the Milwaukee study found
that the utility of value-added analysis declined in the higher grades,
a result that makes perfect sense in light of the fact that a given student's ability to make achievement gains becomes progressively more
dependent on all prior educational experiences, reinforcing the predictions about the cumulative challenges of experience raised in
chapter 2.

In contrast to the Tennessee and Milwaukee studies, however,
other studies of states that had implemented value-added systems
prior to the passage of No Child Left Behind have found that wealthier school communities fare better than students in poorer communities, raising concerns that value-added systems will lead to the same
kinds of disincentives for schools and teachers to serve traditionally
underperforming students.[16]

In use, value-added models have raised some new issues and
requirements—in particular, some nontrivial methodological challenges.[17] To fully implement a VAA system, state agencies require a

considerable amount of demographic data for each student, and this data must be measured with as little error as possible.[18] Doing so requires at least yearly testing of all students, tracking and recording the scores of individual students as they progress through a school or move to a new one, and test compatibility across grade levels.[19] These agencies must decide which data are important to measure.[20] Is, for example, a student's race important because race by itself determines achievement, or is race a proxy for resource inequalities? In addition, many details would have to be worked out and contingencies anticipated, such as what to do if the fifth-grade test is so much harder than the fourth-grade test that every school looks like it is detracting from rather than adding to children's education during that year.

Minnesota has jumped on the value-added bandwagon, and although VAA has not yet become part of Minnesota's compliance with No Child Left Behind, it will soon be incorporated.[21] In March 2004, the Minnesota Office of the Legislative Auditor recommended that the state's Department of Education devise a "plan that outlines how value-added measures of student achievement could be incorporated into the annual AYP determination process."[22] Later that year, Governor Tim Pawlenty encouraged state education officials to take up the recommendations: "As a state, it's time to move to the next level of accountability in our schools. Based on new technologies, we now have the ability to measure individual students compared to where they were the year before. I have instructed the Department of Education to move forward in developing and implementing this 'value-added' system."[23] Minnesota lawmakers followed suit in 2004, requiring state education officials to "include, by the 2006–2007 school year, a value-added component to measure student achievement growth over time."[24]

Minnesota state officials have based their value-added hopes on the promising results of Tennessee's efforts in implementing value-added measures in comparing schools based on the quality of the instruction that they provide. I lack value-added data from Minnesota that can be matched to my survey results because Minnesota does not yet employ VAA in its No Child Left Behind compliance. Future researchers might, however, want to incorporate the theoretical perspective employed here in looking at the future VAA systems that are sure to emerge under No Child Left Behind. A few of the school principals whom I interviewed offered, without prompting, the idea of a growth or value-added model measure of educational achievement as a possible fix for the law:

> We need to embrace longitudinal factors and readiness if we are to measure true success of schools. Someone must have derived a model formula of how to do so somewhere.

> I would expect as the AYP focuses more on student achievement, there will be a "value added" element that eventually teachers will need to respond to should students not improve from the prior year. Not to punish them, but to make them aware of individual student performance on these tests, on attendance, and on graduation rates. The district employees are in this together to help children succeed.

Missing from the recent wave of enthusiasm for VAA systems is a sufficiently detailed discussion of how the results of these regressions will be used. Theoretically, the idea makes a lot of sense; however, implementation makes the idea much trickier. State administrators initially offered VAA as a means to reward schools. With this goal in mind, it is a much more straightforward approach, although it may have inequitable consequences given recent findings that wealthier districts fare better under VAA systems. Much less thought has been given to the implementation of VAA in a system that relies solely on punishment.

A frequent argument in favor of value-added analysis is that it aims to get inside the "black box" of schools, but this is not quite the case. Rather, value-added analysis uses statistical techniques to shake the black box until the educational quality falls out. Where VAA attempts to use these techniques to measure educational quality, I have had much more modest objectives: making a case for the argument that quality does in fact lurk within these test scores. The question is whether "quality" can be measured more directly rather than shaken out of the black box. This is the third, as yet undiscussed, possibility for quality assessment under No Child Left Behind.

A Production Model of Quality Assessment

The production model of evaluation that I propose for inclusion in NCLB is nothing more than an attempt to incorporate principals' and teachers' actions into an accountability system. Rather than jumping through statistical hoops, which bring in a lot of noise and their own problems, to extract a measure of school quality from student test scores, this model is based on the premise that the quality of the principalship should be measured as directly as possible.

For guidance in devising a production model of educational assessment, I turn to several sources. The first is the effective schools literature discussed in chapter 2. Ronald Edmonds and his successors found that effective schools were characterized by safety and order, clear expectations, and strong leadership. To this, it is useful to add the recognition that schools constitute learning communities and that, as in all communities, high levels of trust and interconnectedness are crucial. Cultures, communities, and organizations that are characterized by these high levels of trust and reciprocity are said to possess high levels of "social capital."[25]

In education, the idea of focusing on the conditions of production has its roots in arguments in favor of developing "process indicators" of school performance, an approach that recognizes the fact that "schools provide educational opportunity; they do not directly produce learning."[26] The process approach in education identifies the importance of teacher and curricular quality and the critical role that nonschool factors play in producing academic achievement; however, it has placed less emphasis on school principals' role in maintaining effective school communities and has not been proposed in a system as consequential as No Child Left Behind.

Finally, I add studies of U.S. criminal justice policy by James Q. Wilson and John J. DiIulio Jr. In thinking about the problem of measuring the quality of services provided by those involved with the criminal justice system—individuals with the same high levels of autonomy and discretion that seem to confound top-down educational policymakers—DiIulio, a political scientist, proposed a "new paradigm"[27] for evaluating quality in the criminal justice system that was based on incorporating those closest to the production process into the system of assessment. In addition to high levels of discretion, the criminal justice system shares with the educational system a need to recognize culture and climate in producing quality services. The "broken windows" model of police reform recognizes that police officers in the field are part of local cultures and societies, rejects attempts to dictate behavior from the top down, and realizes that successful police work can often be better observed in good relationships and orderly communities than with arrest data alone.[28]

Measuring production differs fundamentally from measuring outcomes.[29] It involves attention to the types of details that only a student of incentives and bureaucratic minutiae could appreciate. DiIulio's approach and that of his colleague, Charles H. Logan, was to translate an agreed-upon set of goals for these kinds of organizations and to use detailed surveys of those who deliver and receive services to measure attainment of these objectives.[30] The key to DiIulio's and Logan's suggestions was grounding assessment in the conditions of production: "Realistic measures account for the daily activities of justice agencies and for the constraints under which they operate."[31] Performance measures are no panacea, but they can—if accompanied by carefully designed sanctions and rewards—have meaningful consequences for the behaviors of the targeted agents. The trick is to align the assessment and the consequences with the ultimate goals. As DiIulio cautions, "Be careful of what you measure, for you may (or may not) get it."[32]

These ideas are consistent with the theoretical underpinnings of experiential organizations but also point out a few issues that any production model of assessment will inevitably encounter when applied to institutions such as schools, police departments, and prisons whose outputs and outcomes are measured imperfectly if at all. Organizations subject to customer choice do not face the same challenges and ambiguities as those subject to bureaucratic evaluations. They do not have the time. Customers choose. Firms respond. This is the logic behind charter schools and many other forms of public school choice. In the absence of bottom-up control, however, those aspects of production measured at the "micro-level," are likely to be among the few valid measures of police performance."[33] This requirement extends beyond the narrow scope of criminal justice agencies, and

Wilson explicitly connects the challenges and promises of the use of performance measures in criminal justice policy to the illogic of using test scores—with their multiple causative factors—and the promise of the apparently neglected effective schools literature.

I have, in a sense, come full circle, back to the conditions of effective schools; now, however, the conditions of schools are themselves quality measures rather than precursors to quality assessed by other means. A production model of assessing educational quality would, therefore, incorporate detailed surveys of students, teachers, and parents. These surveys would be used to measure the quality of leadership; the commitment to high standards and a focused curriculum; the maintenance of a safe, orderly, and inquisitive environment; and the involvement of parents in school processes.

When asked about how their leadership should be measured, the small group of Minnesota principals interviewed pointed nearly unanimously toward some sort of system based on observing and measuring the quality of what they do. Even the principal of one of Minnesota's most successful schools had a broader sense of measuring the actual conditions of production in his school:

> I believe there are numerous ways to measure my leadership. Do I have a good rapport with my staff? Do my students respond to my leadership?

His sentiments were echoed by the principal of an elementary school with large percentages of students of minority ethnicity and eligible for free or reduced-price lunch. Though his school has avoided AYP identification so far, the fact that only two-thirds of his students scored at Minnesota's level of proficiency on the last round of tests makes future sanction a near certainty without a dramatic and sustained rise in test scores.

> Academic testing needs to be one of the tools. I have no qualms with [Minnesota's] testing. I do believe there must be a better way than testing in March and returning the scores in June. One of my favorite quotes came from a workshop about ten years ago. I don't remember the speaker but he said, "Remember, cows don't gain weight while on the scales."

Assessment should be constant and should be directly tied to lesson or instructional design. Putting kids in special testing settings, interrupting instruction for four days and then returning the results four months later in order to get [a] meaningful test score is pretty unreliable. Here are some other assessment tools to measure leadership:

1. Administrative evaluation by the superintendent. After all, he/she is the boss.
2. Staff surveys. Teachers and non-certified staff.
3. Parent surveys. Ask them how well they think they (parents) are informed.
4. Student surveys. Depending on age of child.
5. Administrative achievement checklists. Let administrators work towards achievement goals just like students.
6. Student achievement checklists like Work Sampling.

Others agreed that the assessment of educational quality can only occur in the actual settings where that quality is produced:

[Spend] real time in an elementary building, follow me around for a day or two, talk with parents, look at our School of Excellence improvement plan, talk to teachers, see where we were 3 years ago and see where we are today.

For some, the culture of the school itself provides a measure of educational quality. The principal of a K–6 school in a relatively low-income neighborhood who had twenty-three years of experience as a teacher believed that test scores were not capable of measuring the kind of leadership that had brought her school, in spite of its challenges, to a five-star ranking:

One aspect that is provided in our school that is not able to be tested is the social/emotional component. We spend a good deal of time working with students to build self-esteem and socially acceptable behaviors. This must be done to bring children to the teachable moment. This cannot be measured in a test.

If you are looking at the administrative leadership of a school you cannot see that in a score. There are things to consider such as a successful working environment where there is a positive atmosphere and staff members' efforts are met with mutual respect. You also must consider communication skills with the staff, students, parents, and community. Finally, there is the matter of professionalism. There are policies to be followed, performance under physical and mental stress, decision making, and commitment to improving the quality of educational programs. Few of these can be assessed by the test scores of students.

Another five-star principal concurred:

I am not sure but measuring confidence, self esteem, commitment to others, world perspective, service to society, respect for the environment would be a better test of leadership. I have a five-star school in reading and math and I pray these other areas are also 5 stars.

A critical worry that a few principals expressed is that the failure to measure educational quality in its entirety—excluding the social conditions within the schools—will damage the school culture itself. These worries echo the predictions of the theory of experiential organizations laid out in chapter 2: that experience matters to quality but that a system of measurement has the potential to change the school's experience.

I spend much less time on non-mandated endeavors that do not show real time benefits, but are important to the overall culture and climate of our school. This includes consensus building, system reform, vision and team building, character education and at-risk programs. As the principal of a K–12 school with an enrollment of about 400 I end up taking a little away for everything. I feel the overall impact has been to move us backward, not forward. We are losing the intangibles that make this school special.

Our test scores were quite good this year (given the socio-economics (reality) of our community) and for that we are very pleased. Two areas were exceptional—reading and writing; and one area, math, was okay compared to the state, but not as good as reading and writing. We will celebrate our successes and continue to work on improving our weaker areas and helping those students that need more help. But, we are realistic enough to know that while proficiency is an admirable goal for every student, it is not worth changing the culture of a school from one that is filled with the "joy of learning" to one that emphasizes results based on test scores alone.

The kind of approach that I propose—if used in combination with traditional outcome measures and if accompanied by meaningful consequences—offers several advantages over the use of outcome measures alone. First, by broadening the range of school quality indicators, it might mitigate the worst of the narrowing effects of test-based accountability in that principals and teachers would no longer have incentives to focus only on a narrow part of the curriculum, itself a narrow part of the education that students receive. This approach would broaden the incentives focus to include much more of what the schooling experience is actually about. In addition, "even though we do not fully understand how schools produce the results that they want, context information may provide clues to policy makers about why we get the outcomes we do."[34] In this way, production indicators potentially constitute a powerful tool for making more sense of the test-based data that we collect. Finally, it may be possible to draw quality distinctions among schools in low-income communities, a process that is not possible when the only indicator—success or failure under AYP—has already or will very soon condemn all inner-city schools to the same failure category.

The Conditions of Educational Production in Minneapolis

To explore the possibility of incorporating production measures of school quality into No Child Left Behind, I turn to a slightly different but related set of data from the Minneapolis Public Schools. As part of a yearly self-evaluation, each spring Minneapolis administrators conduct surveys of students, teachers, and staff about school conditions.[35] The data for this analysis combine the results of the 2003–4 Minneapolis School Information Report with the same AYP, demographic, and test score data used earlier. This analysis thus uses more direct data than I used previously. I relied on indirect measures up to this point because national policymakers have not yet decided that measuring the processes of education as the outcomes is important, thereby resulting in a lack of sufficient data.[36]

The Minneapolis public schools, like their counterparts in other American cities, are failing to make AYP at an alarming rate. Every one of Minneapolis's regular middle and high schools in the district survey failed to make AYP in 2004, and the results for the city's elementary and combined elementary/middle schools were not much better (table 8). Minneapolis, like other large urban centers, also has disproportionately large high-need student populations, not only a challenge under NCLB but also a population of students that desperately needs the law to work. As in the rest of the country, many of the city's schools are progressing quickly down the AYP path, with more than 20 percent of its schools already in at least the second year of sanction as of 2004. Presuming that quality differences exist in the educations students receive in Minneapolis's various middle and high schools, then NCLB is not doing a very good job at distinguishing between the best and the worst of the city's public schools.

TABLE 8.   Adequate Yearly Progress in Minneapolis, 2004

Percentage of Minneapolis public schools that failed to make AYP in 2004	
Elementary	51%
Combined elementary/middle	80%
Middle	100%
High	100%
Percentage of students in Minneapolis public schools who were . . .	
Of minority race and/or ethnicity	73%
Eligible for free or reduced-price lunch	61%
In special education	13%
LEP	24%

Source: Author's analysis based on data from Minnesota Department of Education 2003c, 2003d, 2003f, 2004d.

In this analysis, the Minneapolis survey responses serve as the basis for school production indicators in four categories: safety and discipline, curriculum and high standards, parental involvement, and social capital. The safety and discipline indicator is the average (for each school) of the percentage of "students who say that they are [not] often kept from doing their work by students who misbehave," the percentage of "classroom teachers who are [not] often kept from teaching because of student misbehavior," and the percentage of "students who feel safe in their building."[37] The curriculum and standards indicator is the average of the percentage of "classroom teachers who agree there is a high rate of consistency in how their school's curriculum is implemented across classrooms, and across grade levels," the percentage of "classroom teachers who agree that homework policies/practices among teachers are consistent at their school," and the percentage of classroom teachers who agree that they are "able to incorporate the state high standards into the . . . curricula and in their instruction." The parental involvement indicator is the percentage of "classroom teachers who report sixty percent or more of the students' families attend teacher conferences." Finally, the social capital indicator is the average of the percentage of "students who believe that students in this school show respect for the teachers," the percentage of "students who believe that the teachers in this school treat them with respect," the percentage of "students who agree that their teachers have high expectations for them," and the percentage of "students who trust the adults in this school to keep them safe."

I will use only elementary and combined elementary-middle schools for the rest of the analysis because all of the middle and high schools surveyed failed to make AYP in 2004, thereby providing little information regarding the relationship between school performance indicators and success or failure under No Child Left Behind. I am not concerned with the overall level of satisfaction on the part of students and teachers but with whether these measures of school conditions offer any help in predicting academic achievement and, therefore, with their viability as objective measures of school quality.

Figure 15 presents the results of the same kinds of simulations as I presented earlier, focusing this time on the predicted probability

Probability of a School Making AYP in Minneapolis, 2004

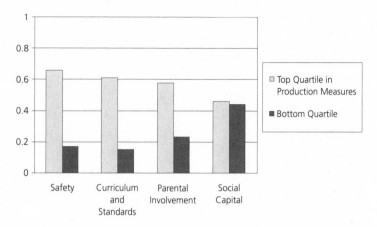

Fig. 15.   AYP failure and the conditions of educational production in Minneapolis. (Data from Minneapolis Public Schools 2004; demographic and AYP data from Minnesota Department of Education 2003c, 2003d, 2004a.)

that a Minneapolis elementary or combined elementary/middle school will make AYP depending on how well the school fared on the student and teacher evaluations of the conditions of production within the school. In other words, the simulation results in figure 15 allow us to consider the effects of better conditions of production on the probablity of AYP success, controlling for the many influences on test scores and outcomes that principals and teachers cannot control. The data lack direct evaluations by parents, though these would be a necessary addition to a collection of school production indicators. As before, regression results are presented in the appendix.

The simulations and the underlying regressions present striking results. The quarter of Minneapolis's regular elementary and combined elementary/middle schools whose principals achieved the highest levels of parental involvement, focus on standards, and safety and discipline were between two and a half and three times as likely to make AYP than the schools in the lowest quartile. All three of these relationships are statistically significant, which is remarkable given the small sample size in these analyses. The social capital variable is not significant, though it would seem almost essential to have a measure of social capital that included data on parental–public school trust, which these data lack.

The diversity of Minneapolis's urban school system has survived suburbanization better than the schools in many other cities. Even within such a system, the concern arises that the results in figure 15 capture only the fact that a number of Minneapolis's public schools are wealthier and less diverse, score higher on many of the production indicators, and made AYP only because of their community characteristics. In other words, perhaps figure 15 illustrates only different patterns of principalship in different communities, not the effects of that leadership on a school's success or failure. If that were the case, then these results would offer little of value to educational policymakers.

A considerable amount of variation exists in Minneapolis's schools, both in the percentages of minority students that they enroll and in the scores that these schools received on student and teacher evaluations of educational production within the schools (table A14). The two most significant differences between the four groups of Minneapolis public schools are the percentages of minority students that they enroll and the levels of parental participation that they observe. These findings are consistent with what we know about resource inequalities and participation in politics and within schools.[38]

Figure 16 presents the simulated results of the same underlying regression models as in figure 15, but this time the quarter of Minneapolis elementary and combined elementary and middle schools that had the lowest percentages of minority students have been deleted from the data set. Although part of the Minneapolis school system, these schools are located in urban enclaves with higher home prices and long lines at the school information fairs that the school district holds every year. Their neighborhoods are characterized not by liquor stores and check-cashing facilities but by boutiques, coffee shops, and organic food.

Two things are remarkable about the results in figure 16. First, given a sample size of only forty-two schools, any of the underlying differences between the best- and worst-scoring schools on my production indicators are significant, which they are for all but the social capital measure. Second, excellent leadership appears to matter

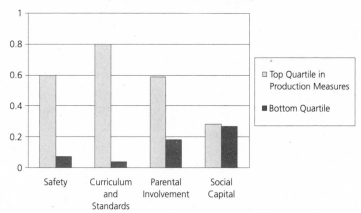

Fig. 16. **Producing quality in Minneapolis's neediest schools. (Data from Minneapolis Public Schools 2004; demographic and AYP data from Minnesota Department of Education 2003c, 2003d, 2004a.)**

more for lower-income schools than for those schools gifted with students who know more about privilege than about deprivation.

Principals of Minneapolis's public schools with the strongest focus
on curriculum and standards—as determined by the evaluations of
students and teachers—are twenty times more likely to make AYP
than those schools with the lowest levels of safety and discipline.
Those schools with the highest levels of safety and discipline were
more than eight times as likely to make AYP, while those that did the
best job of involving their parents were three times as likely to make
AYP.[39] Those schools that failed in these three areas were almost certain to fail to make AYP. These findings confirm what Edmonds and
those who followed him predicted: effective schooling has the greatest benefit in the schools that need it the most.

Conclusions

Test scores at best measure only indirectly what we really care about
in education. No Child Left Behind seeks to create a group of princi-

pals and teachers who focus on what really matters in education: maintaining a safe and orderly environment, reaching out to and involving the parents, and guiding the curriculum by setting an overall tone of high expectations and by having excellent teachers and letting them do their jobs. No matter what kinds of machinations we undertake to extract these realities from test score results, we will always be doing so in a way that is less than perfect. Perhaps most troubling about No Child Left Behind, the law exhibits a lack of faith in the ability of those closest to educational production—teachers, principals, parents, and students—to tell us about the quality of education in their schools, opting instead to place this power in the hands of those very far from the experience of educational quality.

As I have shown, however, another possibility exists, and it has deep roots in thinking about schools and can avoid many of the unintended consequences of No Child Left Behind's indiscriminate nets. Critical readers may challenge the assertion that we should incorporate production measures into NCLB's assessment regimen on the grounds that because leadership can matter for AYP success and failure, perhaps we should stick with what we have. However, the models in these analyses control for community characteristics and compare schools within similar communities. NCLB currently does neither of these things. Rather, I conclude with some confidence that if leadership matters—even within a rigid framework such as No Child Left Behind—then we can use more direct measures of leadership to make quality assessments between schools in similar communities without condemning the public schools of an entire city to sanction and closure. The system of assessment and identification proposed here—to return to the analogy with which I began my empirical investigations in chapter 3—is dolphin friendly. It has the potential to keep the best public, charter, and alternative schools out of our nets and, if we are bold enough, to reward their principals and teachers for performance under pressure. We can make No Child Left Behind work, but doing so will require no small amount of humility, dispassionate analysis, and creativity. We need to get back to the basics of educational quality.

CHAPTER 6

Carrots, Sticks, and Unbroken Windows

Making NCLB Live Up to Its Promises

> If we are to make use of what we knew in Dewey's day
> (and know even better today) about how the human
> species best learns, we will have to start by throwing
> away the dystopia of the ant colony, the smoothly
> functioning (and quietly humming) factory where
> everything goes according to plan, and replace it with
> a messy, often rambunctious, community, with its mul-
> tiple demands and complicated trade-offs.
>
> *Deborah Meier,* Educating a Democracy

The measurement of educational quality is as messy and complicated as education itself. But it is not impossible, and it would be a mistake to wave our hands and assume that No Child Left Behind cannot be fixed. The law undoubtedly constitutes a flawed vehicle, but it makes the kinds of promises to our most disadvantaged citizens and their children worthy of a great liberal democracy. Making NCLB work is worth the effort. As Gary Orfield of the Harvard Civil Rights Project has argued, "What is sorely needed now is an acknowledgment that the too-hasty compromises and contradictions [of NCLB] need to be sorted out, that experts in implementing deep educational change and people who know what the reasonable expectations for progress are and how to measure progress in a more sophisticated way be brought into the process."[1]

In chapter 2, I argued that experience is everything in education. It shapes success, failure, assessment, and compliance. Those closest to the production process know its quality better than anyone else, though even their assessments will never be perfectly accurate. Incentives constitute an important part of the story as well. Given the limitations on principals' and teachers' time resources, any high-stakes accountability plan must be formulated with careful attention to the bureaucratic responses to and unintended consequences of its evaluations and menu of consequences.

Chapter 3 introduced the empirical data for the analyses: a 2003 survey of Minnesota's public and charter school principals on their leadership, their influence, and No Child Left Behind. Combining these results with data on student characteristics, test score results, and adequate yearly progress (AYP) status, I found a troubling though unsurprising relationship between a school's success and failure under No Child Left Behind and the characteristics of the student population. However, principals' leadership decisions can matter under NCLB's test-based regime, offering encouragement that educational outcomes are not determined by socioeconomic status alone.

Chapter 4 turned the analysis around, looking at the effects of being labeled as a failing school on principals' behaviors under and attitudes toward No Child Left Behind. Troublingly, AYP identification does not appear to be associated with a reenergized and refocused principalship but with risk aversion and a loss of influence. I also examined principalship in charter schools, whose dependence on customer preferences—according to the theory laid out in chapter 2—offers inducements toward a more proactive and customer-focused principalship. Though Minnesota's charter schools have a startlingly high AYP failure rate, it may well result from the effects of NCLB's status model of quality assessment rather than from deficiencies in the charter school principalship. I concluded by questioning the logic of denying traditional public schools the benefits of an incentive structure that combines bureaucratic autonomy with a more stakeholder-focused leadership.

In chapter 5, I discussed three alternatives to NCLB's status approach to quality assessment: growth, value-added, and production models of measurement. Though more data are needed, patterns of success under growth models appear to differ from and be preferable to what we see under the current status approach. Charter schools would likely do better under either alternative, as would many traditional public schools with large percentages of minority students and of students eligible for free and reduced price-lunch that were doing the kinds of things that excellent schools do.

I then turned to data from the Minneapolis Public Schools, incorporating the results of parent and student surveys into my larger data set of AYP success and failure along with student and school characteristics. These investigations produced striking results. Though the Minneapolis Public Schools displayed a very high rate of failure—not unlike many urban school systems around the country—schools whose students and teachers felt them to be safe and orderly, focused on curricular standards, and characterized by relatively high levels of parental involvement were much more likely to make AYP than those whose students and teachers reported lower levels of these conditions. These results were even stronger when Minneapolis's relatively advantaged schools were deleted from the analysis, confirming that getting things right in education matters most to those who need it the most.

This chapter moves from questions to answers, taking these lessons as a basis to argue for specific policy proposals as we move forward under No Child Left Behind or whatever state and national policies survive it. I take it as a given that the world of high-stakes top-down accountability is here to stay and offers a series of progressively substantial modifications to the law, from small tweaks to bigger changes in thinking about the prospect of effective and thoughtful educational accountability in the United States.

Having explored issues involved with top-down and bottom-up reforms in education, I would like to propose something more along the lines of a "middle-out" model for fixing No Child Left Behind.[2] The central premise behind middle-out reform is to work from the inside out, basing assessments and incentives on the experiences and insight of those who know what is good and not good and what needs to be done to improve the situation. A plan for incorporating middle-out reform into an accountability system under No Child Left Behind would be based on the following four assumptions and would be undertaken according to the following dictums:

1. Proximity matters; therefore, go inside.   Middle-out reform begins and ends with those closest to the point of production. This is critical in experiential organizations. Assessments and consequences should be based on the wisdom of those who best know quality, including producers and consumers of the services. Both quantitative and qualitative data will be necessary, as will careful attention to any consequences—intended and unintended—of introducing or modifying the incentive structures under which principals and teachers work.

2. Context matters; therefore, be flexible.   One size does not fit all, and those closest to production have much to offer when designing assessments and consequences. In addition, any one measure of quality will probably be insufficient in an undertaking as complex as producing high-quality education.

3. Incentives matter; therefore, be theoretically grounded.   Incentives will be responded to, gamed, and possibly undermined if those involved in the enterprise reject the foundations of the logic behind the incentives. The primary danger with incentives is not that some individuals will game the system (which they will) but that incentive structures may unintentionally reallocate principals' and teachers' time away from aspects of their jobs that we do not wish them to ignore. Multitasking is one of the defining characteristics of principalship. Any incentive structures must be designed with an understanding that time is not an infinite resource.

4. Resources matter; therefore, be bold.   Money does matter, but not uniformly and without careful thought into where it goes and on what basis it is handed out. Resources applied or withheld without an adequate understanding of agency, incentives, leadership, and context will probably not produce the desired educational benefits. The challenges involved in translating these resources into positive outcomes should not lead policymakers to give up on their possibility. Standardized tests have existed for more than a century; however, we as a society have never committed to providing the same level of resources to our poorest students as wealthy individuals have been willing and able to spend on the education of their children. Resources need to be provided based on evidence of success and tailored to sustaining increases in quality, and these rewards should be both financial and bureaucratic.

The effective schools movement may have failed to achieve all of its goals partly because of a lack of a theoretical paradigm that could compete with the simple (and perhaps simplistic) assumptions of those who argued that given the determinacy of student and peer characteristics, resources never matter in education. The insights of scholars of bureaucratic agency offer powerful theoretical tools for developing a policy that allows for the judicious application of rewards and positive incentives. However, we should not be overly optimistic about the instantaneous prospects for any initiative, as many educational reforms have foundered on the shoals of unrealistic expectations.[3] Rather, we need to create a dynamic that feeds on itself and builds toward lasting and sustainable change.[4] Such a system might involve four modifications (in order of increasing significance) of No Child Left Behind.

1. We need to continue to explore the incorporation of growth and value-added models of assessment into AYP calculations, but we should not expect either to be a quick fix to NCLB's problems.

The incorporation of either growth or value-added models of assessment into NCLB is the low-hanging fruit of educational policy in this country, and we are already seeing considerable movement on these fronts. Neither approach, however, is as easy as it sounds. Policymakers should continue to explore the use of these alternate testing formats but should place much more emphasis on implementation than on methodological advantages. Though much discussion has occurred on the merits of either a growth model or a value-added model, scholars have focused much less on what to do with this information or on the important policy issues that need to be addressed prior to large-scale implementation of either a growth or a value-added assessment model.

The main issue is whether one of these alternatives will be used alone or in combination with NCLB's current status model for determining AYP. I would guess that the result will be a combination. If we were to adopt only a growth or value-added model of assessment, then wealthy schools might be sanctioned in roughly the same disproportion as poorer and high minority schools under the status model given that students at more advantaged schools would probably be starting from a relatively high level of achievement. The political implications of such a scenario are easy to imagine and make it easy to dismiss this prospect as unlikely ever to see the light of day.

I start with the assumption that policymakers incorporate a status model and a simple growth model in their evaluations of schools, that (for the sake of simplicity) only academic proficiency (and not attendance and graduation are included), and that all schools succeed in all test participation categories. Four categories of schools would result:

1. those that failed to show both academic proficiency and sufficient gains in proficiency;
2. those that failed to show proficiency but showed yearly gains in proficiency;
3. those that displayed proficiency but failed to show gains; and
4. those that showed both proficiency and gains in proficiency.

Schools in categories 1 and 4 are straightforward: those in category 1 would fail, while those in category 4 would pass. Schools in category 3 would also likely avoid sanction, as most of them would be in wealthier areas with politically active parent communities that would act to shape the policy regulations of such a system.

Therefore, policymakers would be left to decide what to do with those schools that failed to make academic proficiency but displayed strong gains for all students. These schools probably are also failing specific subgroups of students or else the schools would have made safe harbor. One possibility would be to extend safe harbor to the top gaining schools for one year but not the next. Given how much test score gains bounce around from year to year, however, it is not clear that such exemptions would be based on meaningful data. If we exempt from sanction only those schools that make gains for all of their failing subgroups, then nothing will really change, since most of these schools would be making safe harbor. If, conversely, we exempt schools that show gains in proficiency overall but not necessarily in every subgroup, then we run the risk of giving too much leeway to schools that are failing their students in specific subgroups of race, ethnicity, wealth, and ability—that is, exactly the students that No Child Left Behind was designed to help. This is quite a conundrum indeed.

If we were to adopt a value-added system in combination with a status model, the situation would differ slightly but remain complicated. One could imagine exempting a school from identification if it were adding value to the students overall or especially within underperforming subgroups. Again, schools adding value to students in all subgroups would probably not need any additional help. Therefore, both growth models and value-added models sound good in theory, but neither appears to be a magic bullet in practice. At present, only educational methodologists are providing in-depth analyses of these two options. Their ranks need to be supplemented by scholars who pay attention to the important details and consequences of these good ideas.

2. *Choice options, including charter schools, need to be dealt with on a fundamental level.*

Charter schools are not thriving under No Child Left Behind. However, many of these schools serve high-need student populations and display many of the production characteristics that we are trying to encourage with No Child Left Behind. It is more than a little ironic that we feel the need to apply top-down sanctions to a group of schools designed to be free from excessive regulation. Policymakers need to address this contradiction. If we believe in the power of consumer choice, then we should place our faith in it. If not, then we should admit that we are just fumbling around as best we can. Given the complexity of the task, a bit of humility might be useful.

One researcher has advised that a "two-year grace period may be desirable before starting the clock on sanctioning new charters,"[5] given the dual challenges of getting schools started and avoiding sanction under NCLB. While such a plan has the benefit of giving charters a chance to succeed, it runs the risk of ignoring the achievement of the students in these charters. It is also a deeper issue than when or even if we should apply NCLB's assessments and consequences to charter schools. It is not at all clear that more than a fraction of the parents presented with choice options (including charter schools) under NCLB choose any of these options. And if all eligible parents decided to use these options, it is not at all clear that successful schools would have enough seats for all these children.

The real question is whether we are going to treat all parents in the same way under No Child Left Behind, not whether we will provide choices to a lucky few. Parental involvement is beneficial, as is bureaucratic autonomy. We now need to figure out how to bring those benefits into NCLB's framework. If we believe in the simultaneous power of parental evaluations of school quality and bureaucratic autonomy as a reward for this parent-centeredness, then we should consider extending the bureaucratic advantages of charter schools to all public schools.

3. *We need to incorporate a production model of quality assessment into No Child Left Behind.*

I recommend that we adopt a production model of quality assessment while refining the test-based models currently in use or under consideration. A production model of assessment would rely on surveys of students, teachers, and parents to determine the quality of the processes and conditions of education. There is nothing revolutionary about incorporating parent and teacher satisfaction surveys into an evaluation system.[6] However, such input usually offers little more than window dressing for the real test-based accountability provisions. The difference with what I propose here is that parent, teacher, and student surveys would be directly incorporated into the system and that the results of these surveys would have meaningful consequences for schools.

An important task in considering alternative assessment systems under NCLB is to take a look at what school principals think about measuring the quality of their leadership and therefore the quality of their schools. Because I have suggested that we incorporate surveys of teachers, parents, and students into such a system, it makes sense to ask whether principals think that these actors would constitute effective evaluators of school quality. The comments in the follow-up interviews discussed already suggest that such may be the case. Table 9 presents principals' evaluations of which measures of performance most accurately gauge how principals are fulfilling their obligations as leaders and as local school managers. As table 9 clearly demonstrates, Minnesota's traditional public school principals felt that evaluations by the teachers at their schools represented the most effective measures of their performance. These results held true for principals whose schools made AYP in 2003 but were even stronger for those whose schools did not make AYP. For principals of charter

TABLE 9.   Most Effective Measures of Leadership: Minnesota's Principals' Views

	Regular Public (made AYP in 2003) (1)	Regular Public (failed to make AYP in 2003) (2)	Charter School (3)
Test scores of students at this school	13%	14%	8%
Evidence of parent outreach (mailings, events, telephone contacts)	6%	6%	5%
Results of parent satisfaction surveys	16%	16%	28%
Evaluations by teachers at this school	29%	35%	25%
Evaluations by administrative superiors in this district	13%	12%	n.a.
A combination of factors	12%	10%	18%
Other	11%	8%	18%
Number of responses	870	51	40

Source: Minnesota Schools Survey 2003. AYP data from Minnesota Department of Education 2003b. Totals may not add to 100% due to rounding.

Note: The survey question was worded as follows: "Which of the following measures of school performance do you feel *most effectively measures your leadership* as principal of this school?"

n.a. = not applicable.

schools, parent evaluations were the most commonly cited best measure; however, teacher evaluations came in a close second.

This is an important finding, as it points to a divergence in focus between the traditional public and charter school principalships. Principals in traditional public schools may be more inwardly focused, looking for confirmations of their successes and failures within their teaching staffs, while charter school principals look outward to their parent communities for these verdicts.

These results are also consistent with the findings from chapter 4: principals in traditional public schools felt that their power and influence were most effective when they were exercised in concert with rather than in opposition to their teachers. These findings do not presuppose a perpetually happy principal-teacher relationship but assume only that principals and teachers are most effective when their interests are aligned. I am not aware of proposals for modifying No Child Left Behind to incorporate teachers' evaluations of principals into assessments of school performance. It is difficult, however, to imagine a private-sector system that fails to incorporate subordinates' assessments of their managers in assessing whether those managers are performing adequately. For some reason, this is typically the case in public education.

Roughly 10 percent of the principals in the Minnesota survey took the option of writing in their own responses to the question of most effective measure of leadership rather than circling an item from the menu that I provided (the "other" category in table 9). Table 10 presents the results of these write-in responses, with charter and noncharter schools combined, given the small number of respondents.

The second-most-common response was something that should have been included in the menu and a factor that showed up consistently in the follow-up interviews: evaluations by students. Students are the primary stakeholders in education, yet their feedback is excluded entirely from No Child Left Behind's evaluation and their potential role in creating a comprehensive system of incentives for schools is completely ignored. I, like many of my fellow researchers, failed to listen carefully enough to what the theory was telling me, unwittingly contributing to the omission of students from the accountability process even though they are causes as much as examples of achievement.[7]

No one is closer to the production of educational quality than the students. Even elementary school children have useful feedback to offer to assess the conditions of educational production, as the coherence and consistency of student evaluations and academic performance in the Minneapolis data attest. Students know if they feel safe, if they are allowed to concentrate in class, if their teachers care about them, and if their teachers care about the material. The proponents of the "breaking ranks" model of educational accountability reject the current situation whereby "the student's role in the educational process is passive and subordinate,"[8] replacing it with a model of "student-centered accountability"[9] that recognizes the critical role that school climate and culture play in educational excellence.

The most commonly offered measure of principals' leadership in the responses in table 10 was a combination of teacher, parent, and student evaluations—that is, precisely the types of measures I advocate for use in modifying No Child Left Behind's assessment regimen. Many of the Minnesota principals who chose to offer their opinions about effective measures of their leadership felt that student evaluations should be a component of a more comprehensive system

TABLE 10.   Other Effective Measures of Leadership: Minnesota's Principals' Write-in Responses

	All Principals
Student evaluations	17%
Combination of parent, teacher, and student evaluations	20%
School climate and student engagement	10%
Goal attainment and mission orientation	11%
Gain models, value-added models of test scores	9%
Attendance, graduation, and postgraduation success	13%
Reputation, word of mouth	5%
Other	15%
Number of responses	109

Source: Minnesota Schools Survey 2003. AYP data from Minnesota Department of Education 2003b. Totals may not add to 100% due to rounding.

Note: The survey question was worded as follows: "Which of the following measures of school performance do you feel *most effectively measures your leadership* as principal of this school?"

of evaluation. Several also placed the utility of these evaluations within an understanding of the school as a social system producing whole citizens. Nonprompted measures of superior leadership included the following:

> If students like school, feel safe, feel as though they have input into decision-making, are challenged academically, and are good citizens to each other.

> School climate/school success on scores *and* student interest/belief in education. [It] has to be well-rounded—nothing [in the list] related to student perceptions.

> Student success factors such as participation in leadership activities, student satisfaction, student self-efficacy, student personal growth, student confidence, belief in self.

> Building relationships and trust with staff, students, and parents.

We know what principals think. They agree with the core prediction of the theories that I have discussed in this book: those closest to the production of education are best able to assess its quality. The question, of course, is how to incorporate these evaluations and assessments into No Child Left Behind's test-based world.

4. The implementation of No Child Left Behind must incorporate meaningful rewards into its accountability system.

At its core, No Child Left Behind is a punitive system despite the fact that its passage was associated with a promise of a significant boost in federal education funding and that its implementation has resulted in more monies for Title I (though somewhat less than was promised). Nevertheless, there are no federal rewards for schools that succeed under the law other than keeping its wolves at bay.[10] In addition, relatively little discussion has examined the role that incentives, positive or negative, play in evaluating No Child Left Behind's implementation and the likelihood of it's success or failure:[11]

"Unfortunately, the prevailing mind-set among too many politicians and policy makers is something right out of *Field of Dreams:* 'If we set high standards, students will magically achieve.' "[12]

One superintendent interviewed as part of the 2004 study by Minnesota's Office of the Legislative Auditor summed up the irony of NCLB's punishment-driven philosophy: "If research drives this law, then those who promulgated it know that punishment is the least likely way to get improvement. Yet the only form of motivation for teachers and schools is the threat of loss of revenue, prestige, and the school itself."[13]

This aspect of No Child Left Behind is very difficult to reconcile with a true desire on the part of its authors to make public schools succeed. Any reasonable exploration of bureaucratic agency raises serious questions about an incentive structure built only on avoiding punishment. Given what James Q. Wilson has observed about coping organizations and what I have found about the experiential subset of these organizations, NCLB seems almost designed to produce mediocrity, risk aversion, and doing time. The empirical results of this book support this baffling conclusion. Therefore, in addition to incorporating alternative measures of educational excellence and thinking more carefully about choice, policymakers must incorporate meaningful rewards into their plans.

Table 11 presents the responses by public school principals in Minnesota to a question about the most effective incentives for improving academic achievement within their particular schools. What is striking about these results is how similar they are among different groups of principals. These individuals do not report that they want more money for themselves; rather, they seek the resources necessary to achieve their vision for excellence within their schools. Of course, it is possible that these principals are merely providing what they think is the "correct" answer to the question. Nevertheless, all the groups agree, and their observations concur with the findings of this study. Public school principals are strategic actors, and they see the potential utility or necessity of making their institutions more responsive to the needs and wishes of their parents and students; however, they desire the resources to allow them to do so. Perhaps a theoretically and empirically sound accountability program could help make this a reality.[14]

Table 12 summarizes the responses of principals who chose, in a separate question, to offer their views on what other kinds of incentives might be offered to principals who demonstrated superior performance. Resources for the school (not for the principal) again dominated. Increased funding for smaller class sizes as well as resources for training were commonly suggested. However, not all principals felt that incentives were necessary, pointing to the limitations on any incentive system put into place in an endeavor where much of the motivation is intrinsic, but even these individuals might benefit from more and better leadership tools.

Several of the principals who offered their own opinions saw bureaucratic rewards as effective additions to resource rewards. Such bureaucratic enticements might include more autonomy—not necessarily power over teachers, just the power to shape the teaching team. The principal of one of Minnesota's wealthiest metro-area high schools wanted authority not to fire his teachers but to recruit and keep them. In response to the question, "What other potential incentives that were not mentioned in the above list do you think might be

TABLE 11. Incentives for Superior Leadership: Minnesota's Principals' Views

	Regular Public (made AYP in 2003) (1)	Regular Public (failed to make AYP in 2003) (2)	Charter School (3)
Cash bonuses	6%	6%	6%
Recurring salary increases	12%	2%	6%
Sabbatical leaves	2%	6%	9%
Decreased oversight from state and local administration	14%	20%	21%
Additional support staff	66%	65%	56%
Number of responses	810	48	34

Source: Minnesota Schools Survey 2003. AYP data from Minnesota Department of Education 2003b. Totals may not add to 100% due to rounding.

Note: The survey question was worded as follows: "Of the following incentives that might be offered to public school principals for superior performance, which do you think is the *most likely to improve academic achievement* within the school?"

offered to public school principals who exhibit superior performance?" he requested,

> Choosing a certain percentage of teachers to hire or keep
> employed even if they do not meet licensing requirements. I
> have had to let high quality people go in order to satisfy union
> and licensing demands. Without a doubt, these people had an
> outstanding effect on student achievement.

The desire for flexibility in hiring and retention—politically a much
easier task than flexibility in firing—concurs with the results of a
2004 study for the Minneapolis Public Schools that advised the district to "increase the latitude of principals to interview, select, and
hire their staff." The authors of a 2003 national study of school and
district accountability also concluded that "high performance can be
rewarded with additional flexibility in school management, additional resources, or group awards or gifts to school employees."[15]

Reclaiming No Child Left Behind's Liberal Agenda

Student, teacher, and parent surveys can be useful measures of the
quality of leadership and therefore the quality of education in our

TABLE 12.   Other Effective Incentives for Superior Leadership: Minnesota's
Principals' Write-in Responses

	Percentage of Write-in Responses
Public recognition for principal, teachers, and/or students	18%
Leaves, vacations, etc.	3%
Fewer regulations in terms of running the school	9%
Paid training and workshops for principals and staff	14%
Other financial benefits (retirement, fringe, etc.)	3%
Increased funding for smaller class sizes, better equipment, etc.	23%
Incentives not necessary	15%
Other	15%
Number of responses	421

Source: Minnesota Schools Survey 2003. Totals may not add to 100% due to rounding.

Note: The survey question was worded as follows: "What other potential incentives that were not mentioned in the above list do you think might be offered to public school principals who exhibit superior
performance?"

public schools. Incentives—both resource-based and autonomy-based—can be more thoughtfully incorporated into such a system. I conclude this book by offering some ideas on how policymakers might incorporate production-based incentives into No Child Left Behind's ambitious agenda.

The plan would focus on schools in America's urban centers and disadvantaged rural communities. Though the theoretical and empirical investigations undertaken in this book apply equally to all public schools, NCLB focuses on closing the achievement gap between advantaged and disadvantaged students. The plan would be based on combining the results of systematic and comprehensive annual surveys of teachers, students, and parents with the results of the variant of test-based accountability state officials chose to adopt. Results of these surveys would be used in two ways. First, they would be publicized. For schools operating under a system of choice, these results would align the top-down assessment with the bottom-up provision of choice in a way that makes much more theoretical sense than what we are now doing. Second, being labeled as successful would have significant consequences for a school on the NCLB sanction track as well as beyond NCLB's punitive focus.

The heart of the evaluation would be a system that awarded one point to schools serving high-need student populations for each of eight criteria, including having made AYP in the previous year as well as being in the top 25 percent of schools in the comparison group based on

- one-year gains in reading proficiency;
- one-year gains in math proficiency;
- safety and order (as measured by teacher, student, and parent surveys);
- a focus on curriculum and high standards (as measured by teacher, student, and parent surveys);
- creating a climate of respect and trust (measured by surveys of students and teachers);
- a focus on high standards (as measured by surveys of parents and teachers); and
- parental involvement (parental attendance at conferences and rate of volunteerism).

Schools would be compared to other schools in the state with similar sociodemographic characteristics. The top 20 percent of these schools, based on their point scores, would be identified as "schools of promise" and would get placed on a timeline of rewards that resembled No Child Left Behind's current timeline of sanctions. These rewards would be cumulative, just like the sanctions for AYP failure. Rewards under this system, however, would be both financial and bureaucratic and would be funded by the federal government, but not out of previously allocated Title I monies. In other words, the plan would entail a commitment of new and dedicated funds, not another reallocation of what has already been appropriated. Table 13 lays out the increasingly significant proposed rewards for repeated identification as a school of promise under this plan.

In the first year of identification, the school's status—along with lists of top-performing schools in each of the point categories— would be made public as part of No Child Left Behind's reporting requirements. In addition, schools of promise that did not make AYP in the same year would not advance on the sanctions schedule but

TABLE 13.   Increasingly Significant Rewards for Schools of Promise

Cumulative Years of Identification	Rewards for Schools
1 year	Identification as a "school of promise" with public notification
	Progression along AYP sanction track frozen for 1 year (if applicable)
2 years	Progression along AYP sanction track reset to year 1 (if applicable)[a]
	School receives one-year grant for paid training and leaves for teachers.[b]
3 years	School given control over hiring and retaining teachers.[a]
	School receives a 10% bonus (based on total staff salaries) to hire additional support staff.[b]
4 years	School receives a 10% bonus (based on total expenditures for teacher salaries) to hire additional teachers to reduce class sizes.[a]
	School exempted from forced layoffs and reassignment of teachers.[b]
5 years	Paid leave time for teachers and principal to conduct workshops at other schools
	Teachers receive a 10% salary bonus.[b]
	Principal eligible for leadership program

[a]Each subsequent year continues rewards from all previous years.
[b]Previous financial rewards continue in future years but are not cumulative. (Amounts are set at first year of award.)

would stay frozen at the previous year's level. The second year of identification would be rewarded with the reset of progress along the AYP sanction track to the first year, if applicable. The school would also receive a one-year grant to allow for paid training and leave for teachers and staff. This grant would recur in subsequent years of identification. The plan would not require consecutive identification to progress along the timetable, though perhaps it would include a reset button if a school failed to achieve promising status again after a number of years.

The third cumulative year of identification would reward schools with control of hiring and retention of teachers. I use the word *school* intentionally here, as I think more thought needs to be given, perhaps at the district or building level, to the relative power of principals and teachers in this reward. Principals need more autonomy in this area; however, one can imagine principal/teacher collaboration as well. In addition, a 10 percent bonus, based on current expenditures on staff, would be granted to the school to hire additional support staff. These funds would be allocated by the principal.

In the fourth year of cumulative identification, the school would receive a 10 percent bonus based on current expenditures on teacher salaries to hire additional teachers to reduce class sizes. Funding for these positions would be guaranteed for a specified number of years, since the uncertainty created by hiring new teachers without some such guarantee would likely nullify any benefits from the initiative. The school would also be exempted from forced layoffs and reassignment for that year, though teachers could still opt to be reassigned under standard district procedures.[16]

In the fifth year of identification, all teachers in the school would receive a 10 percent salary bonus, recurring in each subsequent year that the school was identified as promising. These salary bonuses would continue but would not be cumulative. Principals and teachers in these schools would be compensated, including the hiring of substitute staff, for conducting workshops and training of others in the district or state. In addition, principals would have the option of participating in a leadership program. New funds would be allocated to provide these principals with semester or one-year leaves to mentor other principals in the district or state. Perhaps the selection of individuals to fulfill administrative requirements during the leave could be used as an apprenticeship program for principals and assistant principals from other schools willing to undertake the challenge of leading a public school in a high-need community.

Issues and Concerns

This plan for modifying No Child Left Behind would require a non-trivial amount of data collection; however, this task does not seem overwhelming in comparison to the demands placed on schools and districts to collect and evaluate student achievement test results. In addition, these new data would be useful in their own right. Parents choosing schools, for example, would be very interested in finding out which schools were demonstrating quality in all or some aspects of their production. Principals in promising schools (and even those that just missed identification) could use the data to retain active parents in their school communities in the face of competition from charter schools, public schools in other districts, and possibly even private schools.

As has been discussed, any system of accountability must be carefully analyzed for intended and unintended consequences of the incentive system that it creates, and this caution applies equally well to the production model proposed here. Any approach brings the very real possibility that those subject to its reach will try to game the system to their advantage, perhaps in conflict with the system's ultimate objectives. However, the possibility that principals will reallocate their time to ensure positive survey responses from their parents, students, and teachers might lead to a beneficial skewing of the allocation of principals' time. The goal would not be to get principals to ignore performance on standardized tests but rather to facilitate a greater balance between time and energy devoted to the tests and time and energy devoted to reaching out to parents and fostering a vibrant social community.

Any incentive structure under this system would also ideally be compatible with and complimentary to both top-down and bottom-up reforms, using both carrots and sticks to align principals' and teachers' behaviors with customers' preferences. There is no theoretical basis for denying traditional public schools the benefit—now given only to charter schools—of having an incentive and rewards system geared to becoming more aware of and responsive to parents' wishes and quality evaluations. This lack of attention to customers and autonomy, measurement and sanction represents one of the most critical gaps in current discussions of NCLB's prospects.

Teachers might have incentives to overstate their principal's leadership ability or the status of the school climate, since they would be the recipients of many of these benefits, particularly in later years. The idea, however, is to reward schools with more resources (teachers included) and more autonomy for the principal. Teachers, therefore, would be providing their survey responses with the knowledge that higher scores might contribute to more resources but would also result in the principal having more authority—including over hiring, retention, and the disbursement of grants and leaves. Schools whose teachers were performing well, partly because of the quality of the principalship, would benefit the most. Again, the goal is to strike a balance in the incentive structure.

Any consideration of financial and bureaucratic incentives must be made with dual consideration of feasibility and the fact that many of these rewards may continue beyond the fifth year. Perhaps various reset buttons would force schools to start over on the identification track; however, many of the positive incentives need to be provided with some assurance that they will continue so that school and district officials can prepare accordingly.

This plan is in no way meant to be definitive, and all of the financial incentives would need to be subject to a thorough cost-assessment process. The percentages required for identification have been set with the dual goals of making success possible for schools but not so high as to overwhelm the federal government's ability to fund the program or to make the AYP provisions meaningless. Such an outcome would very likely undercut political support for No Child Left Behind. The key is to strike a careful balance between improving NCLB and killing it. Any system that proposes to identify and reward educational quality should also be subject to intense review, debate, and modification. This plan is no different. My objective is only to help steer the debate away from complaisance or futility and toward action and hope. At the very least, policymakers should seriously consider a pilot project involving a few select cities—with a similarly matched set of control cities—to explore this plan's potential to improve achievement and reenergize and refocus our public schools in the communities that need it the most.

Conclusions

The modern and not-so-modern history of reforming public schooling in the United States is littered with policy proposals that have failed because of a lack of the political will necessary to sustain them over the long haul, a failure to commit sufficient resources to implement them in full, poor planning, or a combination of these factors. No Child Left Behind is an imperfect vehicle, to be sure, but it is noble in its flaws, promising in its failures. No inherent incompatibility exists between high-stakes accountability and educational excellence. Properly devised, high-stakes accountability can have the benefits that we seek.

To make NCLB work, we need to hold schools—or more accurately, those who run and operate them—accountable for factors that they can control and that matter to student achievement yet not hold them accountable for factors beyond their control. We need to distinguish between schools that are failing their students and governments that are failing their schools, sanctioning and starving schools of promise in the communities that most need educational excellence. We must reward those who succeed with the tools, conditions, and resources needed to continue to do their jobs at a high level. This, in my thinking, would be a "fixed windows" approach to educational reform.

The promise to close the achievement gap between advantaged and disadvantaged students in this country has been codified into federal law. The apparatus—though hastily devised and wobbling under the weight of our expectations—is here. The knowledge of where we want to go has been here for a long time. We now need leaders who are unafraid of the inevitable opposition from entrenched interests on either side of the educational reform debate. No Child Left Behind's liberal promises demand and deserve nothing less.

Appendix

TABLE A1.   The Relationship between Diversity, School Size, and AYP Failure in Minnesota, 2003

Subject	Number of Qualifying Subcategories (1)	Number of Schools (2)	Percentage Failing to Make AYP in 2003 (3)	Average School Enrollment (4)
Reading proficiency	1	234	<1%	367
	2	418	4%	443
	3	92	16%	493
	4	68	28%	511
	5	43	40%	543
	6	7	43%	745
Mathematics proficiency	1	236	<1%	367
	2	417	5%	444
	3	91	15%	490
	4	68	28%	511
	5	43	40%	543
	6	7	43%	745

Source: Author's analysis based on data from Minnesota Department of Education 2003b, 2003c, 2003d, 2003f.

Note: Figures are for Minnesota's traditional public schools with either grade three or grade five tested in reading and mathematics. These schools are used because Minnesota did not use test score results to calculate AYP for middle and high schools until 2004. I use 2003 in these tables rather than 2004 as the Minnesota Department of Education currently reports the number of qualifying subgroups only for those schools that failed in 2004. In 2003, these data were reported for all schools, regardless of success or failure under No Child Left Behind.

TABLE A2. Principals' Allocation of Time

	A Great Deal of Time (1)	Time Spent Relative to Other Activities (2)
Facilitating achievement of the school's mission	13%	–6%
Supervising faculty	8%	–3%
Guiding development of the curriculum	5%	–13%
Building relationships with the parent community	10%	no difference
Maintaining the physical security of students and staff	11%	no difference
Managing facilities	9%	–4%
Completing administrative tasks	32%	+25%

Source: Minnesota Schools Survey 2003.

Note: The survey question was worded as follows: "During the past month, about how much of *your time* was spent on the following activities?" Each variable is coded as: 1 "None or almost none," 2 "Slightly less time than on other activities," 3 "About as much time as other activities," 4 "Slightly more time than other activities," 5 "A great deal of time."

Column 1 presents the percentages of principals who reported spending "a great deal of time" on the activity. Column 2 presents the percentage differences above or below the mean amount of time spent by all principals on all activities.

TABLE A3. Leadership in Minnesota's Failing Schools, 2004

	Top Quartile, by Percentage Minority (1)	Bottom Quartile, by Percentage Minority (2)
Percentages of principals who spent a great deal of time on . . .		
Facilitating achievement of the school's mission	16%	11%
Supervising faculty	13%	5%
Guiding development of the curriculum	6%	5%
Building relationships with the parent community	14%	6%
Maintaining the physical security of students and staff	11%	10%
Managing facilities	9%	7%
Completing administrative tasks	31%	29%

Source: Minnesota Schools Survey 2003.

Note: The question item was worded as follows: "During the past month, about how much of *your time* was spent on the following activities?" Each variable was coded as: 1 "None or almost none," 2 "Slightly less time than on other activities," 3 "About as much time as other activities," 4 "Slightly more time than other activities," 5 "A great deal of time."

TABLE A4. Means and Standard Deviations for Variables in AYP and Five-Star Regression Analyses in Chapter 3

	Mean (1)	Standard Deviation (2)
AYP 2004 failure	0.22	0.42
Five-star school, 2004	0.13	0.34
Rural	0.24	0.42
Percentage minority	0.17	0.21
Percentage free lunch eligible	0.22	0.17
Percentage limited English proficient	0.06	0.10
Percentage special education	0.13	0.04
School enrollment (100s)	5.81	4.23
Highest grade offered (0–12)	7.59	3.00
Average teacher salary ($1,000)	44.62	5.61
Percentage of teachers with master's degree	0.41	0.21
Principal's years of experience	10.35	7.92
Principal's teaching experience	14.33	7.99
Principal has doctorate	0.13	0.34
Time spent on . . .		
Facilitating mission	3.02	1.11
Supervising faculty	3.09	0.92
Guiding curriculum	2.75	0.99
Parent relationships	3.18	0.97
Security	3.18	1.02
Managing facilities	3.04	1.01
Administrative tasks	3.92	0.90

Source: Minnesota Schools Survey 2003. Demographic and AYP data from Minnesota Department of Education 2003b, 2003c, 2003d, 2004a, 2004b.

TABLE A5. Full Results: Five-Star Schools and Failure to Make Adequate Yearly Progress in 2004

	Five-Star School in 2004 (1)	Failure to Make AYP in 2004 (2)
Time spent on . . .		
Facilitating mission	−0.10	−0.08
	(0.06)	(0.06)
Supervising faculty	0.00	0.11
	(0.07)	(0.07)
Guiding curriculum	0.09	−0.17**
	(0.06)	(0.07)
Parent relationships	0.18***	0.00
	(0.06)	(0.07)
Security	−0.17***	0.08
	(0.06)	(0.07)
Managing facilities	−0.04	0.12*
	(0.07)	(0.07)
Administrative tasks	−0.09	−0.03
	(0.07)	(0.07)
Rural	−0.01	0.29*
	(0.15)	(0.15)
Percentage minority	−1.47	3.01***
	(0.93)	(0.70)
Percentage eligible for free or reduced-price lunch	−0.84	0.08
	(0.93)	(0.72)
Percentage LEP	−1.42	0.97
	(2.03)	(1.03)
Percentage special education	−3.94*	7.93***
	(2.07)	(1.67)
School enrollment (100s)	−0.03	0.16***
	(0.02)	(0.02)
Highest grade offered (0–12)	0.01	0.16***
	(0.02)	(0.26)
Principal's years of experience	0.01	−0.02**
	(0.01)	(0.01)
Principal's teaching experience	0.00	0.00
	(0.01)	(0.01)
Principal has doctorate	−0.25	0.01
	(0.18)	(0.18)
Average teacher salary ($1,000)	0.04**	−0.02
	(0.02)	(0.02)
Percentage of teachers with master's degree	0.09	0.73
	(0.40)	(0.48)
Constant	−1.40	−4.55***
	(0.85)	(0.92)
N	877	877
Wald chi^2 (19)	71.00	211.74
Prob > chi^2	0.00	0.00
Pseudo R^2	0.12	0.40

Source: Minnesota Schools Survey 2003. Demographic and AYP data from Minnesota Department of Education 2003b, 2003c, 2003d, 2004a, 2004b.

Note: Column 1 presents probit regression results probability of being labeled a five-star school in 2004. Column 2 presents probit regression results probability of failing to make AYP in 2004. Robust standard error estimates in parentheses.

*p < 0.1;   **p < .05**;   ***p < .01, two-tailed.

TABLE A6. NCLB: What Minnesota's Principals Think

Percentage of Principals Who Feel That
NCLB Will Improve Academic Achievement

Regular public school	56%
Regular public school that made AYP in 2003	56%
Regular public school that failed to make AYP in 2003	59%
Charter school	35%
Top quartile, by percentage minority	67%
Bottom quartile, by percentage minority	49%
Top quartile, by percentage eligible for free or reduced-price lunch	59%
Bottom quartile, by percentage eligible for free or reduced-price lunch	52%

Source: Minnesota Schools Survey 2003. Demographic data from Minnesota Department of Education 2003b, 2003c, 2003d.

Note: The survey question was worded as follows: "What effect do you think the No Child Left Behind Act will have on student achievement?"

Table A7.   Anticipated Effects of NCLB on Principals' Influence in Specific Areas

	Percentage Reporting That No Child Left Behind Will . . .		
	Limit Their Influence (1)	Have No Effect (2)	Enhance Their Influence (3)
Setting performance standards for students at this school	31%	18%	51%
Establishing curriculum at this school	34%	23%	42%
Hiring teachers at this school	16%	66%	18%
Evaluating teachers at this school	8%	69%	23%
Setting discipline policy at this school	6%	81%	12%
Deciding how school budget will be spent	34%	35%	29%

Source: Minnesota Schools Survey 2003. Totals may not add to 100% due to rounding.

Note: The survey question was worded as follows: "During the 2003–2004 academic year, to what extent will the *No Child Left Behind Act* limit or enhance *your influence* on the following policy areas at your school?" Each variable is coded as 1 "Limit very much," 2 "Limit somewhat," 3 "No effect," 4 "Enhance somewhat," 5 "Enhance very much."

TABLE A8. Means and Standard Deviations for the Analyses in Chapter 4

	Mean (1)	Standard Deviation (2)
AYP 2003 failure	0.05	0.23
Charter school	0.04	0.18
Effects of NCLB on student achievement	3.41	0.96
Effects of NCLB on . . .		
Setting performance standards	3.22	1.18
Establishing curriculum	3.05	1.14
Hiring teachers	3.01	0.76
Evaluating teachers	3.16	0.63
Setting discipline policy	3.05	0.52
Deciding how budget is spent	2.90	1.02
Mean of NCLB effects	3.07	0.67
Influence of . . .		
Principal	3.87	0.90
Parents	3.16	0.95
Teachers	3.77	0.91
Minnesota Department of Education	3.87	1.13
Influence of principal on . . .		
Setting performance standards	3.52	1.02
Establishing curriculum	3.27	0.99
Hiring teachers	4.57	0.80
Evaluating teachers	4.69	0.66
Setting discipline policy	4.39	0.68
Spending budget	3.82	1.05
Time spent on . . .		
Facilitating mission	3.00	1.10
Supervising faculty	3.06	0.91
Guiding curriculum	2.72	0.99
Parent relationships	3.15	0.96
Security	3.14	1.02
Managing facilities	3.02	1.02
Administrative tasks	3.93	0.90
Mean time spent	3.15	0.50
Rural	0.23	0.42
Percentage minority	0.18	0.22
Percentage eligible for free or reduced-price lunch	0.23	0.18
Percentage LEP	0.06	0.11
Percentage special education	0.13	0.05
School enrollment (100s)	5.62	4.24
Highest grade offered (0–12)	7.67	3.01
Average teacher salary ($1,000)	44.15	5.86
Percentage of teachers with master's degree	0.40	0.21
Principal's years of experience	10.24	7.87
Principal's teaching experience	14.09	8.02
Principal has doctorate	0.13	0.33
Female principal	0.37	0.48
Minority principal	0.04	0.19
Principal's age	49.00	7.72

Source: Minnesota Schools Survey 2003. Demographic and AYP data from Minnesota Department of Education 2003c, 2003d, 2004a.

TABLE A9. Full Ordered Probit Regression Results: Expected Consequences of NCLB on Principals' Influence

	Mean Influence (1)	Performance Standards (2)	Curriculum (3)	Evaluating Teachers (4)	Discipline Policy (5)	Hiring Teachers (6)	Setting Budget (7)
Failure to make AYP in 2003	0.12 (0.11)	0.14 (0.21)	-0.37* (0.22)	0.53** (0.24)	0.40 (0.26)	0.002 (0.19)	-0.26 (0.23)
Charter school	-0.34** (0.15)	0.01 (0.21)	-0.01 (0.20)	-0.23 (0.32)	0.01 (0.36)	-0.41 (0.29)	0.20 (0.20)
Mean effect of NCLB on influence	—	2.85*** (0.13)	3.12*** (0.20)	1.88*** (0.12)	1.38*** (0.12)	1.81*** (0.12)	2.30*** (0.09)
Rural	-0.07 (0.06)	0.01 (0.10)	-0.33*** (0.10)	0.04 (0.11)	0.02 (0.13)	0.14 (0.10)	0.06 (0.10)
Percentage minority	-0.22 (0.28)	0.07 (0.45)	-1.08*** (0.38)	-0.10 (0.44)	0.47 (0.50)	0.67* (0.40)	-0.16 (0.40)
Percentage eligible for free or reduced-price lunch	0.23 (0.21)	0.35 (0.39)	0.36 (0.36)	-0.50 (0.46)	-0.94* (0.52)	-0.04 (0.44)	-0.19 (0.40)
Percentage LEP	0.01 (0.38)	-0.68 (0.74)	1.10* (0.65)	0.18 (0.65)	-0.43 (0.73)	-1.22* (0.65)	1.27* (0.73)
Percentage special education	-0.09 (0.08)	-0.59 (0.62)	-0.04 (0.61)	1.60* (0.93)	-0.08 (1.00)	-0.50 (0.83)	0.78 (0.66)
School enrollment	-0.005 (0.007)	0.01 (0.01)	-0.01 (0.01)	0.01 (0.01)	-0.01 (0.01)	-0.003 (0.018)	-0.002 (0.012)
Highest grade offered (0–12)	-0.02** (0.01)	-0.01 (0.02)	0.04*** (0.01)	-0.02 (0.02)	-0.04** (0.02)	0.02 (0.02)	-0.01 (0.01)
Principal's years of experience	-0.006 (0.004)	-0.012* (0.008)	-0.01 (0.01)	0.00 (0.01)	-0.01 (0.01)	0.01 (0.01)	0.00 (0.01)
Principal's teaching experience	-0.001 (0.003)	-0.012* (0.006)	0.00 (0.01)	0.00 (0.01)	-0.02* (0.01)	0.014** (0.006)	0.01 (0.01)
Principal has doctorate	-0.09 (0.08)	-0.03 (0.12)	0.04 (0.13)	0.00 (0.13)	-0.06 (0.16)	-0.19 (0.14)	0.06 (0.11)

	(1)	(2)	(3)	(4)	(5)	(6)	(7)
Female principal	0.11**	−0.07	−0.05	0.20*	0.13	0.05	−0.02
	(0.05)	(0.09)	(0.10)	(0.11)	(0.12)	(0.10)	(0.09)
Minority principal	0.40**	−0.29	0.12	0.86***	0.30	−0.25	0.06
	(0.18)	(0.28)	(0.24)	(0.22)	(0.34)	(0.26)	(0.27)
Principal's age	0.004	0.01	0.01	0.00	0.01	−0.004	−0.01
	(0.004)	(0.01)	(0.01)	(0.01)	(0.01)	(0.009)	(0.01)
Average teacher salary ($1,000)	−0.01	−0.003	−0.02*	0.00	0.00	0.01	0.00
	(0.01)	(0.010)	(0.01)	(0.01)	(0.01)	(0.01)	(0.01)
Percentage of teachers with master's degree	0.18	0.24	0.05	−0.05	−0.61*	0.26	0.06
	(0.16)	(0.27)	(0.30)	(0.33)	(0.33)	(0.29)	(0.26)
N	912	912	912	912	912	912	912
Wald chi² (18)	—	508.38	350.04	306.87	163.82	333.60	603.95
Prob > chi²	—	0.00	0.00	0.00	0.00	0.00	0.00
Pseudo R^2	($R^2 = 0.04$)	0.42	0.47	0.37	0.28	0.31	0.36
Cutpoint 1 (constant)	(3.46)	5.79	6.27	2.19	1.10	3.40	4.34
Cutpoint 2	—	7.55	8.28	3.57	1.94	4.51	5.99
Cutpoint 3	—	8.64	9.75	7.02	5.66	7.51	7.72
Cutpoint 4	—	11.20	12.43	9.30	7.40	8.93	9.79

Source: Minnesota Schools Survey 2003. Demographic and AYP data from Minnesota Department of Education 2003c, 2003d, 2004a.

Note: The survey question was worded as follows: "During the 2003–2004 academic year, to what extent did the *No Child Left Behind Act* limit or enhance *your influence* on the following policy areas at your school?" Each variable is coded as 1 "Limit very much," 2 "Limit somewhat," 3 "No effect," 4 "Enhance somewhat," 5 "Enhance very much."

Column (1) presents OLS regression results. Columns 2–7 present ordered probit regression results. Robust standard error estimates in parentheses. — = not applicable.

*$p < 0.1$;   **$p < .05$**;   ***$p < .01$, two-tailed.

TABLE A10. Full Ordered Probit Regression Results: Influence of Principal in Policy Areas

	Performance Standards (1)	Curriculum (2)	Evaluating Teachers (3)	Discipline Policy (4)	Hiring Teachers (5)	Setting Budget (6)
Failure to make AYP in 2003	-0.59*** (0.16)	-0.47*** (0.15)	-0.02 (0.19)	-0.24 (0.17)	-0.32 (0.21)	-0.04 (0.16)
Charter school	0.40* (0.23)	0.18 (0.28)	-0.49* (0.29)	-0.51** (0.24)	-0.34 (0.29)	0.31 (0.22)
Effects of NCLB on influence	0.25*** (0.06)	0.15*** (0.06)	0.04 (0.07)	0.08 (0.06)	0.01 (0.06)	0.16*** (0.06)
Rural	-0.17* (0.09)	0.03 (0.09)	0.03 (0.12)	-0.13 (0.10)	-0.07 (0.11)	-0.11 (0.09)
Percentage minority	0.79* (0.41)	-0.54 (0.44)	0.84* (0.49)	0.71* (0.41)	0.50 (0.47)	1.32*** (0.43)
Percentage eligible for free or reduced-price lunch	-0.26 (0.38)	0.76* (0.45)	-1.46*** (0.47)	-1.03*** (0.40)	-1.88*** (0.47)	-1.29**** (0.43)
Percentage LEP	-0.41 (0.60)	0.36 (0.55)	-0.66 (0.70)	0.26 (0.62)	-0.26 (0.67)	-0.16 (0.62)
Percentage special education	-0.27 (0.90)	0.20 (0.75)	0.41 (0.86)	-0.12 (0.89)	0.24 (0.82)	-0.17 (0.85)
School enrollment	-0.018 (0.014)	-0.017 (0.013)	0.02 (0.02)	-0.01 (0.01)	0.07*** (0.02)	0.03*** (0.01)
Highest grade offered (0–12)	0.018 (0.014)	0.05*** (0.01)	-0.02 (0.02)	0.01 (0.02)	-0.03* (0.02)	-0.06*** (0.01)
Influence of . . .						
Parents	0.13*** (0.05)	0.10** (0.05)	0.00 (0.06)	-0.06 (0.05)	-0.08 (0.06)	0.01 (0.05)
Teachers	0.12** (0.05)	0.27*** (0.05)	0.22*** (0.06)	0.26*** (0.06)	0.38*** (0.06)	0.22*** (0.05)
Minnesota Department of Education	0.08** (0.03)	0.02 (0.03)	0.05 (0.04)	0.09*** (0.04)	0.07* (0.04)	0.04 (0.03)

	(1)	(2)	(3)	(4)	(5)	(6)
Principal's years of experience	0.03***	0.00	0.00	0.01	0.01	0.01
	(0.01)	(0.01)	(0.01)	(0.01)	(0.01)	(0.01)
Principal's teaching experience	0.01	0.00	-0.01	0.01	-0.003	0.00
	(0.01)	(0.01)	(0.01)	(0.01)	(0.007)	(0.01)
Principal has doctorate	0.05	0.13	0.00	0.29**	-0.14	0.15
	(0.12)	(0.13)	(0.15)	(0.15)	(0.16)	(0.13)
Female principal	0.01	-0.17**	-0.09	0.08	0.06	0.13
	(0.01)	(0.08)	(0.10)	(0.09)	(0.11)	(0.09)
Minority principal	0.16	0.67***	0.06	0.29	0.35	0.00
	(0.23)	(0.20)	(0.27)	(0.23)	(0.31)	(0.01)
Principal's age	-0.023***	0.00	0.01	-0.01	-0.004	0.00
	(0.007)	(0.01)	(0.01)	(0.01)	(0.009)	(0.01)
Average teacher salary ($1,000)	0.00	-0.01	-0.03**	-0.02*	-0.05***	0.00
	(0.01)	(0.01)	(0.01)	(0.01)	(0.01)	(0.01)
Percentage of teachers with master's degree	-0.34	-1.14***	0.50	-0.37	0.18	0.20
	(0.28)	(0.28)	(0.33)	(0.29)	(0.33)	(0.27)
N	892	892	892	892	892	892
Wald chi^2 (21)	107.83	200.51	57.63	66.57	163.00	147.30
Prob > chi^2	0.00	0.00	0.00	0.00	0.00	0.00
Pseudo R^2	0.04	0.08	0.04	0.04	0.09	0.06
Cutpoint 1	-1.15	-0.58	-2.70	—	-3.71	-1.34
Cutpoint 2	-0.03	0.72	-2.13	-2.53	-3.03	-0.21
Cutpoint 3	0.86	1.87	-1.60	-1.30	-2.55	0.62
Cutpoint 4	1.93	2.96	-0.71	0.06	-1.64	1.58

Source: Minnesota Schools Survey 2003. Demographic and AYP data from Minnesota Department of Education 2003c, 2003d, 2004a.

Note: The survey question was worded as follows: "How much *actual influence* do you think you *as principal* have regarding the following *policy areas at your school*?" The variables are coded from 1 "No influence" to 5 "A great deal of influence."

Columns 1–6 present ordered probit regression results. Robust standard error estimates in parentheses. — = not applicable.

*$p < 0.1$;   **$p < .05$**;   ***$p < .01$, two-tailed.

TABLE A11.   Full Probit Regression Results: Influence of Actors

	Influence of . . .			
	Principal (1)	Parents (2)	Teachers (3)	Minnesota Department of Education (4)
Failure to make AYP	−0.48**	0.23	0.08	0.53***
in 2003	(0.23)	(0.17)	(0.23)	(0.17)
Charter school	−0.40	−0.05	0.91**	−0.28
	(0.36)	(0.24)	(0.36)	(0.21)
Rural	0.01	−0.21**	0.10	0.01
	(0.10)	(0.09)	(0.10)	(0.09)
Percent minority	0.53	0.32	−0.43	−0.66
	(0.42)	(0.38)	(0.41)	(0.43)
Percentage eligible for free	0.18	−0.63*	0.27	0.04
or reduced-price lunch	(0.43)	(0.36)	(0.41)	(0.43)
Percentage LEP	−0.25	−0.53	0.92	−0.17
	(0.68)	(0.57)	(0.71)	(0.57)
Percentage in special	0.78	−0.88	−0.90	0.31
education	(0.91)	(0.63)	(0.79)	(0.71)
School enrollment	0.02	−0.02**	0.02	0.01
	(0.02)	(0.01)	(0.02)	(0.01)
Highest grade offered	0.00	−0.021	0.00	−0.03**
(0–12)	(0.02)	(0.012)	(0.02)	(0.01)
Influence of . . .				
Principal	—	0.15***	0.94***	−0.12**
		(0.06)	(0.07)	(0.06)
Parents	0.15***	—	0.59***	−0.02
	(0.05)	(0.06)		(0.05)
Teachers	0.99***	−0.68***	—	−0.10
	(0.07)	(0.07)	(0.06)	
Minnesota Department of	−0.06	−0.02	−0.06	—
Education	(0.04)	(0.03)	(0.04)	
Principal's years of	0.00	0.00	0.01	−0.012*
experience	(0.01)	(0.01)	(0.01)	(0.007)
Principal's teaching	0.00	0.00	0.00	0.00
experience	(0.01)	(0.01)	(0.01)	(0.01)
Principal has doctorate	0.04	0.02	−0.04	−0.11
	(0.12)	(0.11)	(0.13)	(0.12)
Female principal	−0.04	0.08	0.22**	0.26***
	(0.09)	(0.08)	(0.09)	(0.08)
Minority principal	0.06	0.36	0.17	0.52***
	(0.28)	(0.24)	(0.29)	(0.27)
Principal's age	−0.014*	0.00	0.00	0.01
	(0.008)	(0.01)	(0.01)	(0.01)
Average teacher	−0.03**	0.00	0.01	−0.01
salary ($1,000)	(0.01)	(0.01)	(0.01)	(0.01)

TABLE A11.—*Continued*

| | Influence of . . . | | | |
	Principal (1)	Parents (2)	Teachers (3)	Minnesota Department of Education (4)
Percentage of teachers with master's degree	0.14 (0.28)	0.14 (0.26)	0.12 (0.27)	−0.09 (0.27)
N	905	905	905	905
Wald chi^2 (20)	321.75	224.68	434.12	73.83
Prob > chi^2	0.00	0.00	0.00	0.00
Pseudo R^2	0.24	0.15	0.31	0.03
Cutpoint 1	−1.66	0.06	2.03	−3.19
Cutpoint 2	0.33	1.78	3.78	−2.23
Cutpoint 3	1.78	3.09	5.35	−1.59
Cutpoint 4	3.46	4.30	7.18	−0.84

Source: Minnesota Schools Survey 2003. Demographic and AYP data from Minnesota Department of Education 2003c, 2003d, 2004a.

Note: The survey question was worded as follows: "How much *actual influence* do you think each of the following has regarding *making decisions that affect your school*?" The variables are coded from 1 "No influence" to 5 "A great deal of influence."

Columns 1–4 present ordered probit regression results. Robust standard error estimates in parentheses. — = not applicable

*$p < 0.1$;   **$p < .05$;   ***$p < .01$, two-tailed.

TABLE A12. Full Ordered Probit Regression Results: Principals' Time Spent on Activities

	Time Spent . . .						
	Facilitating School's Mission (1)	Guiding the Curriculum (2)	Supervising Faculty (3)	Building Relationships with Parent Community (4)	Maintaining Physical Security (5)	Managing Facilities (6)	Completing Administrative Tasks (7)
Failure to make AYP in 2003	-0.45***	0.04	-0.06	0.06	0.30*	-0.04	0.23
	(0.15)	(0.17)	(0.17)	(0.16)	(0.18)	(0.17)	(0.17)
Charter school	0.48**	0.16	-0.61**	0.44*	-0.43**	-0.24	0.19
	(0.22)	(0.24)	(0.24)	(0.23)	(0.20)	(0.24)	(0.24)
Mean time spent on all activities	1.30***	1.31***	1.40***	1.48***	1.73***	1.28***	0.86***
	(0.09)	(0.09)	(0.09)	(0.09)	(0.09)	(0.08)	(0.08)
Rural	-0.07	.014	-0.09	-0.29***	0.08	0.18*	0.05
	(0.09)	(0.09)	(0.09)	(0.09)	(0.09)	(0.09)	(0.09)
Percentage minority	0.53	-0.35	0.57	0.55	0.12	-0.18	-1.28***
	(0.40)	(0.43)	(0.47)	(0.41)	(0.40)	(0.40)	(0.09)
Percentage eligible for free or reduced-price lunch	0.25	0.76*	-0.11	-1.33***	-0.59	-0.03	0.75*
	(0.44)	(0.40)	(0.47)	(0.41)	(0.37)	(0.40)	(0.43)
Percentage LEP	0.74	0.57	0.00	-0.87	-0.29	-0.59	0.72
	(0.56)	(0.55)	(0.73)	(0.61)	(0.66)	(0.63)	(0.63)
Percentage in special education	-0.59	-1.36	-0.34	-1.29	1.80**	1.03	1.14
	(0.98)	(0.94)	(1.09)	(0.98)	(0.91)	(0.96)	(1.00)
School enrollment	0.01	-0.001	0.015	-0.03**	0.01	-0.01	0.00
	(0.01)	(0.010)	(0.011)	(0.01)	(0.01)	(0.01)	(0.01)
Highest grade offered (0–12)	-0.038**	-0.001	0.00	-0.07***	0.07***	0.020	0.02
	(0.015)	(0.014)	(0.01)	(0.01)	(0.01)	(0.015)	(0.02)
Principal's years of experience	-0.015***	-0.001	0.01	-0.01	0.012**	0.01	0.00
	(0.006)	(0.001)	(0.01)	(0.01)	(0.006)	(0.01)	(0.01)
Principal's teaching	-0.013***	0.001	0.00	0.01	0.00	0.01	0.00
	(0.007)	(0.001)	(0.01)	(0.01)	(0.01)	(0.01)	(0.01)

	(1)	(2)	(3)	(4)	(5)	(6)	(7)
Principal has doctorate	0.30***	0.20*	0.07	0.02	-0.15	-0.31***	-0.15
	(0.11)	(0.12)	(0.11)	(0.12)	(0.12)	(0.11)	(0.12)
Female principal	0.03	0.01	0.07	0.03	0.00	-0.23***	0.11
	(0.08)	(0.01)	(0.09)	(0.08)	(0.08)	(0.09)	(0.09)
Minority principal	0.00	-0.12	0.00	-0.15	0.18	0.27	-0.16
	(0.20)	(0.22)	(0.22)	(0.20)	(0.22)	(0.22)	(0.23)
Principal's age	0.024***	0.001	0.00	0.00	-0.01	-0.012*	-0.01
	(0.007)	(0.001)	(0.01)	(0.01)	(0.01)	(0.007)	(0.01)
Average teacher salary ($1,000)	-0.01	-0.002	-0.03***	-0.01	0.02*	0.02*	0.01
	(0.01)	(0.001)	(0.01)	(0.01)	(0.01)	(0.01)	(0.01)
Percentage of teachers with master's degree	0.40	-0.31	0.21	0.65**	-0.73***	-0.27	0.06
	(0.26)	(0.29)	(0.26)	(0.28)	(0.27)	(0.26)	(0.28)
N	882	882	882	882	882	882	882
Wald chi^2 (18)	323.54	284.33	275.73	373.88	431.59	285.89	132.71
Prob > chi^2	0.00	0.00	0.00	0.00	0.00	0.00	0.00
Pseudo R^2	0.14	0.12	0.14	0.17	0.17	0.11	0.06
Cutpoint 1	2.66	2.46	0.73	0.72	4.24	2.60	0.02
Cutpoint 2	4.02	3.94	2.42	2.49	5.60	3.89	1.30
Cutpoint 3	5.16	5.06	3.83	3.79	6.95	5.11	2.62
Cutpoint 4	5.97	6.15	4.97	5.07	8.13	6.15	3.62

Source: Minnesota Schools Survey 2003. Demographic and AYP data from Minnesota Department of Education 2003c, 2003d, 2004a.

Note: The survey question was worded as follows: "During the past month, about how much of *your time* was spent on the following activities?" Each variable is coded as 1 "None or almost none," 2 "Slightly less time than on other activities," 3 "About as much time as other activities," 4 "Slightly more time than other activities," 5 "A great deal of time."

Columns 1–7 present ordered probit regression results. Robust standard error estimates in parentheses.

*$p < 0.1$;   **$p < .05$;   ***$p < .01$, two-tailed.

TABLE A13.   External Measures of Leadership in Minneapolis's Elementary and Combined Elementary/Middle Schools

	Average Score
Safety and discipline	68%
Curriculum and high standards	79%
Parental involvement	69%
Social capital	82%

Source: Author's analysis based on data from Minneapolis Public Schools 2004.

TABLE A14.   Inequality and Production in the Minneapolis Public Schools

	1st Quartile (lowest) (1)	2nd Quartile (2)	3rd Quartile (3)	4th Quartile (highest) (4)
Percentage minority students	41%	71%	86%	97%
Safety and discipline	78%	69%	63%	62%
Curriculum and high standards	83%	83%	74%	76%
Parental involvement	92%	70%	67%	46%
Social capital	87%	84%	83%	74%
Failure to make AYP in 2004	27%	43%	79%	100%

Source: Author's analysis based on data from Minneapolis Public Schools 2004. Demographic and AYP data from Minnesota Department of Education 2003c, 2003d, 2004a.

TABLE A15. Means and Standard Deviations for Variables in Minneapolis School Analysis

	Mean (1)	Standard Deviation (2)
Failure to make AYP in 2004	0.61	0.49
Safety and discipline	67.89	10.42
Curriculum and high standards	78.84	11.10
Parental involvement	68.75	26.08
Social capital	82.07	11.03
Percentage minority	72.84	22.79
Percentage eligible for free or reduced-price lunch	61.56	23.52
Percentage LEP	25.76	14.67
Percentage in special education	11.93	3.83
Combined elementary/middle	0.35	0.48
Enrollment (100s)	4.18	1.84
Average teacher salary ($1,000)	53.7	4.60
Percentage of teachers with master's degree	52.07	12.87

Source: Minneapolis Public Schools 2004. Demographic, AYP, and test score data from Minnesota Department of Education 2003c, 2003d, 2003f, 2004a, 2004d.

TABLE A16. Full Results: AYP in Minneapolis

	Failure to Make AYP in 2004: Minneapolis (1)	Failure to Make AYP in 2004: Minneapolis (without lowest quartile of percentage minority enrollment) (2)
Safety and discipline	−0.11***	−0.15***
	(0.04)	(0.06)
Curriculum and standards	−0.09**	−0.26***
	(0.04)	(0.09)
Parental involvement	−0.04***	−0.055**
	(0.01)	(0.025)
Social capital	0.06	0.07
	(0.04)	(0.04)
School enrollment (100s)	0.03	−0.40
	(0.21)	(0.34)
Average teacher salary ($1,000)	0.37***	0.83***
	(0.13)	(0.30)
Percentage of teachers with	−0.12***	−0.17***
master's degree	(0.04)	(0.07)
Percentage minority	−0.05	0.03
	(0.04)	(0.08)
Percentage eligible for free	0.04	0.03
or reduced-price lunch	(0.03)	(0.05)
Percentage LEP	0.00	0.00
	(0.02)	(0.03)
Percentage in special education	−0.16*	−0.13
	(0.09)	(0.12)
Combined elementary/middle	1.08	3.97**
	(0.89)	(1.56)
Constant	1.75	−7.39
	(6.81)	(9.63)
N	53	41
Wald chi^2 (12)	34.13	23.57
Prob > chi^2	0.00	0.02
Pseudo R^2	0.45	0.62

Source: Minneapolis Public Schools 2004. Demographic and AYP data from Minnesota Department of Education 2003c, 2003d, 2003f, 2004a, 2004d.

*$p < 0.1$;   **$p < .05$;   ***$p < .01$, two-tailed. Robust standard error estimates in parentheses.

Notes

1. The Best-Laid Plans

1. Alfred Powers and Howard McKinley Corning, eds., *History of Education in Portland* (Portland, OR: WPA Adult Education Project, 1937); David B. Tyack, *The One Best System: A History of American Urban Education* (Cambridge: Harvard University Press, 1974).

2. Powers and Corning, *History of Education in Portland*, 47. Also cited in Tyack, *The One Best System*, 47.

3. Tyack, *The One Best System*, 48, citing Powers and Corning, *History of Education in Portland*, 327.

4. Powers and Corning, *History of Education in Portland*, 51.

5. Tyack, *The One Best System*, 48.

6. Linda Darling-Hammond, "From 'Separate but Equal' to 'No Child Left Behind': The Collision of New Standards and Old Inequalities," in Deborah Meier and George Wood, eds., *Many Children Left Behind* (Boston: Beacon Press, 2004); Gail L. Sunderman and Jimmy Kim, *Inspiring Vision, Disappointing Results: Four Studies on Implementing the No Child Left Behind Act* (Cambridge: The Civil Rights Project, Harvard University, 2004). Jack Jennings observes, "One could say, therefore, that the new law uses conservative means to achieve liberal ends" ("Stricter Federal Demands, Bigger State Role: What to Expect From the No Child Left Behind Act," *State Education Standard*, 2002), 26; The Education Commission of the States recommends that policymakers "embrace NCLB as a civil rights issue" ("ECS Report to the Nation: State Implementation of the No Child Left Behind Act"), vii.

7. National Conference of State Legislatures, *Task Force on No Child Left Behind: Final Report* (Washington, DC: National Conference of State Legislatures, 2005), 5. Richard Murnane argues that higher standards are "critical to reducing educational inequalities that have left many American families with

insufficient earnings to support their children" (*The Impact of School Resources on the Learning of Inner City Children* [Cambridge, MA: Ballinger, 1975], 57). Gary Orfield states that in "many ways, [NCLB] is the most startling departure in federal educational policy in American history" (Sunderman and Kim, *Inspiring Vision, Disappointing Results*), 1.

8. 20 U.S.C. § 6301 (Pub. L. 107-110). For a good overview of the law, see Peter W. D. Wright, Pamela Darr Wright, and Suzanne Whitney Heath, eds., *Wrightslaw No Child Left Behind* (Hartfield, VA: Harbor House Law Press, 2003).

9. Douglas N. Harris and Carolyn D. Herington, "Accountability, Standards, and the Growing Achievement Gap: Lessons from the Past Half-Century," *American Journal of Education* 111, no. 2 (2006): 210.

10. 20 U.S.C. § 6301. Frederick M. Hess comments on the likely weakening of these teeth over time, as political forces coalesce to oppose and water-down the law ("Refining or Retreating? High-Stakes Accountability in the States," in Paul E. Peterson and Martin R. West, eds., *No Child Left Behind? The Politics and Practice of School Accountability* [Washington, DC: Brookings Institution Press, 2003]).

11. 20 U.S.C. § 6301.

12. *San Antonio Independent School District v. Rodriquez,* 411 U.S. 1 (1973).

13. Center on Education Policy, *From the Capital to the Classroom: Year 3 of the No Child Left Behind Act* (Washington, DC: Center on Education Policy, 2005). As of 2002, roughly 58 percent of U.S. public schools in the United States received Title I funds, for an average of $472 per low-income student (U.S. Department of Education, Office of the Undersecretary, Elementary and Secondary Education, *No Child Left Behind: A Desktop Reference* [Washington, DC: U.S. Department of Education, Office of the Undersecretary, Elementary and Secondary Education, 2002]).

14. 20 U.S.C. § 6311. States are not required to apply the sanctions under No Child Left Behind to public schools with fewer than 35 percent of their students eligible for Title I funds.

15. No Child Left Behind uses these census categories for students of nonmajority ethnicity.

16. Center on Education Policy, *From the Capital to the Classroom;* Jason Pierce, "Minimum Size of Subgroups for Adequate Yearly Progress (AYP)" (Education Commission of the States, 2003).

17. John R. Novak and Bruce Fuller, *Penalizing Diverse Schools? Similar Test Scores, but Different Students, Bring Federal Sanctions* (Stanford: Policy Analysis for California Education Brief, 2003).

18. Ninety-five percent of all students and students within each subgroup must take the test, allowing for accommodations on test-day for students with special needs (20 U.S.C. § 6311).

19. Minnesota Office of the Legislative Auditor, "Evaluation Report: No Child Left Behind" (St. Paul: Program Evaluation Division, 2004), 30; see also National Association of Elementary School Principals and National Association of Secondary School Principals, *K–12 Principals Guide to No Child Left Behind*

(Alexandria, VA: National Association of Elementary School Principals and National Association of Secondary School Principals, 2003).

20. 20 U.S.C. § 6311.

21. The students with disabilities or with limited English proficiency can be offered reasonable accommodations when they take the tests (20 U.S.C. § 6311).

22. 20 U.S.C. § 6311.

23. Schools and districts are allowed to apply alternate measures of proficiency for the 1 percent of their most disabled student populations, though this is the subject of current and constant negotiations between states and the federal government.

24. 20 U.S.C. § 6311.

25. States are allowed one-year waivers in the event of "a natural disaster or a precipitous and unforeseen decline in the financial resources of the State" (20 U.S.C. § 6311).

26. 20 U.S.C. § 6316.

27. U.S. Department of Education, *No Child Left Behind: A Desktop Reference.*

28. 20 U.S.C. § 6316.

29. U.S. Department of Education, *No Child Left Behind: A Desktop Reference,* 17.

30. 20 U.S.C. § 6316.

31. 20 U.S.C. § 6316.

32. 20 U.S.C. § 6316.

33. Jennifer L. Hochschild and Nathan Scovronick, *The American Dream and the Public Schools* (New York: Oxford University Press, 2003).

34. Andrew Rudalevige, "No Child Left Behind: Forging a Congressional Compromise," in Paul E. Peterson and Martin R. West, eds., *No Child Left Behind? The Politics and Practice of School Accountability* (Washington, DC: Brookings Institution Press, 2003); Paul Manna, "Leaving No Child Behind," in Christopher T. Cross, ed., *Political Education: National Policy Comes of Age* (New York: Teachers College Press, 2004).

35. Center on Education Policy, *From the Capital to the Classroom.*

36. Ibid., vii.

37. John G. Cronin, Gage Kingsbury, Martha S. McCall, and Branin Bowe, "The Impact of the No Child Left Behind Act on Student Achievement and Growth: 2005 Edition" (Lake Oswego, OR: Northwest Evaluation Association, 2005). The authors caution that students for whom scores can be obtained over time tend to have more stable enrollment patterns and therefore may be more likely to have higher academic achievement.

38. Ibid.

39. Alfie Kohn, *The Case Against Standardized Testing: Raising the Scores, Ruining the Schools* (Portsmouth, NH: Heinemann, 2000); Deborah Meier, "NCLB and Democracy," in Deborah Meier and George Wood, eds., *Many Children Left Behind: How the No Child Left Behind Act Is Damaging Our Children and Our Schools* (Boston: Beacon, 2004); Joel Packer, "No Child Left Behind and Academic Yearly Progress—Fundamental Flaws: A Forecast for Failure," paper presented at

the Center on Education Policy Forum on Ideas to Improve the Accountability Provisions under the No Child Left Behind Act, Washington, DC, 2004; George Wood, "A View From the Field: NCLB's Effects on Classrooms and Schools," in Meier and Wood, *Many Children Left Behind.* Deborah Meier writes that the current push for accountability "decreases the chances that young people will grow up in the midst of adults who are making hard decisions and exercising mature judgment in the face of disagreements" ("Educating a Democracy," in Joshua Cohen and Joel Rogers, eds., *Will Standards Save Public Education?* [Boston: Beacon, 2000]), 5. Lorraine McDonnell explores the political struggles that standardized testing often produces in *Politics, Persuasion, and Educational Testing* (Cambridge, MA: Harvard University Press, 2004).

40. Hess, "Refining or Retreating?"

41. Meier, "Educating a Democracy," 4.

42. Ibid., 7–9.

43. Darrel Drury and Harold Duran, "The Value of Value-Added Analysis," *National School Boards Association Policy Brief* 3, no. 1 (2003); Eric A. Hanushek and Margaret E. Raymond, "Lessons about the Designs of State Accountability Systems," in Paul E. Peterson and Martin R. West, eds., *No Child Left Behind? The Politics and Practice of School Accountability* (Washington, DC: Brookings Institution Press, 2003); Gavin Payne, "The Implementation of the Accountability Provisions of the No Child Left Behind Act," paper presented at the Center on Education Policy Forum on Ideas to Improve the Accountability Provisions under the No Child Left Behind Act, Washington, DC, 2004.

44. Paul A. Herdman, Nelson Smith, and Harold Doran, "Value-Added Analysis: A Critical Component of Determining Adequate Yearly Progress" (*Charter School Friends Network Policy Brief,* 2002); National Conference of State Legislatures, *Task Force on No Child Left Behind: Final Report.*

45. Drury and Doran, "The Value of Value-Added Analysis."

46. Novak and Fuller, *Penalizing Diverse Schools?* See also Darling-Hammond, "From 'Separate but Equal' to 'No Child Left Behind'"; Thomas J. Kane and Douglas O. Staiger, "Unintended Consequences of Racial Subgroup Rules," in Paul E. Peterson and Martin R. West, eds., *No Child Left Behind? The Politics and Practice of School Accountability* (Washington, DC: Brookings Institution Press, 2003).

47. Robert L. Linn, "Rethinking the No Child Left Behind Accountability System," paper presented at the Center on Education Policy Forum on Ideas to Improve the Accountability Provisions under the No Child Left Behind Act, Washington, DC, 2004, 3 (emphasis is the author's). See also W. James Popham, *America's "Failing" Schools: How Parents and Teachers Can Cope with No Child Left Behind* (New York: RoutledgeFalmer, 2004).

48. See Daniel Koretz, "Limitations in Use of Achievement Tests a Measures of Educators' Productivity," *Journal of Human Resources* 37, no. 4 (2002); Robert L. Linn, Eva L. Baker, and Damian W. Betebenner, "Accountability Systems: Implications of Requirements of the No Child Left Behind Act of 2001," *Educational Researcher* 31, no. 6 (2002); Robert L. Linn, Eva L. Baker, and Stephen B. Dunbar, "Complex Performance-Based Assessment: Expectations and Validation Criteria," *Educational Researcher* 20, no. 8 (1991).

49. Alfie Kohn asserts that the "whole [accountability] movement is rooted

in a top-down, ideologically driven contempt for public institutions" (*The Case Against Standardized Testing: Raising the Scores, Ruining the Schools* [Portsmouth, NH: Heinemann, 2004]), 91.

50. Jeffrey L. Pressman and Aaron Wildavsky, *Implementation: How Great Expectations in Washington Are Dashed in Oakland* (Berkeley: University of California Press, 1984).

51. Center on Education Policy, *From the Capital to the Classroom;* National Conference of State Legislatures, *Task Force on No Child Left Behind: Final Report.*

52. Steven D. Levitt, *Freakonomics: A Rogue Economist Explores the Hidden Side of Everything* (New York: Morrow, 2005).

53. James E. Ryan, "The Perverse Incentives of the No Child Left Behind Act," *NYU Law Review* 79, no. 3 (2004).

54. United States General Accounting Office, *No Child Left Behind Act: Improvements Needed in Education's Process for Tracking States' Implementation of Key Provisions*, (Washington, DC: United States General Accounting Office, 2004), 3.

55. Payne, "The Implementation of the Accountability Provisions of the No Child Left Behind Act"; Popham, *America's "Failing" Schools.*

56. United States General Accounting Office, *No Child Left Behind Act: Improvements Needed in Education's Process for Tracking States' Implementation of Key Provisions.*

57. Minnesota Office of the Legislative Auditor, *Evaluation Report: No Child Left Behind*, 36.

58. Julian R. Betts and Anne Danenberg, *The Effects of Accountability in California*, in Paul E. Peterson and Martin R. West, eds., *No Child Left Behind? The Politics and Practice of School Accountability* (Washington, DC: Brookings Institution Press, 2003); Michael Casserly, "Choice and Supplemental Services in America's Great City Schools," in Frederick M. Hess and Chester E. Finn Jr., eds., *Leaving No Child Behind? Options for Kids in Failing Schools* (New York: Palgrave Macmillan, 2004); Jane Hannaway and Kendra Bishoff, "Florida: Confusions, Constraints, and Cascading Scenarios," in Hess and Finn, eds., *Leaving No Child Behind?;* William Howell, "Fumbling for an Exit Key: Parents, Choice, and the Future of NCLB," in Hess and Finn, eds., *Leaving No Child Behind?*; Robert Maranto and April Gresham Maranto, "Options for Low-Income Students: Evidence from the States," in Hess and Finn, eds., *Leaving No Child Behind?*

59. Center on Education Policy, *From the Capital to the Classroom;* See also Gary Orfield's Introduction in Sunderman and Kim, *Inspiring Vision, Disappointing Results.*

60. W. James Antle III, "The Bull That Never Ends," *American Conservative*, 1 August 2005.

61. *Pontiac v. Spellings*, 05-CV-71535-DT (2005).

62. 20 U.S.C. § 7907.

63. United States General Accounting Office, *Unfunded Mandates: Analysis of Reform Act Coverage* (Washington, DC: United States General Accounting Office, 2004), 22. See also "First National Suit over Education Law," *AP Newswire*, 20 April 2005. A Michigan U.S. District Court has since dismissed the suit; the dismissal is being appealed (Toni Locy, "Judge Tosses Out NCLB Lawsuit," *Minneapolis Star Tribune*, 23 November 2005).

64. National Conference of State Legislatures, *Task Force on No Child Left Behind*, vi.

65. Ibid., vii.

66. National Conference of State Legislatures, *Task Force on No Child Left Behind;* see 20 U.S.C. § 7861.

67. 20 U.S.C. § 7904.

68. 20 U.S.C. § 7905.

69. Center on Education Policy, *From the Capital to the Classroom.*

70. George Archibald, "Utah Set to Reject No Child Left Behind," *Washington Times,* 23 February 2005; Ronnie Lynn, "Utah Bucks Feds on Schools," *Salt Lake Tribune,* 20 April 2005.

71. Lynn, "Utah Bucks Feds on Schools."

72. National School Boards Association, "Education Vital Signs," *American School Board Journal,* February 2006, 1.

73. Hanushek and Raymond, "Lessons about the Designs of State Accountability Systems."

74. Education Commission of the States, "ECS Report to the Nation"; Hanushek and Raymond, "Lessons about the Designs of State Accountability Systems"; Linn, "Rethinking the No Child Left Behind Accountability System"; Herdman, Smith, and Doran, "Value-Added Analysis"; National School Boards Association, "NSBA's Bill to Improve No Child Left Behind," *Priority Issue,* January 2005.

75. Linn, "Rethinking the No Child Left Behind Accountability System," 4.

76. Center on Education Policy, *From the Capital to the Classroom;* Packer, "No Child Left Behind and Academic Yearly Progress—Fundamental Flaws."

77. Linn, "Rethinking the No Child Left Behind Accountability System." The National School Boards Association has recommended that the *N* size for a group within a school be increased to a percentage of that school's total enrollment to better measure achievement in schools with large enrollments and that the safe harbor requirements be reduced from 10 to 5 percent growth ("NSBA's Bill to Improve No Child Left Behind").

78. Center on Education Policy, *From the Capital to the Classroom;* Linn, "Rethinking the No Child Left Behind Accountability System."

79. Darling-Hammond, "From 'Separate but Equal' to 'No Child Left Behind'"; Jennifer Hochschild, "Rethinking Accountability Politics," in Paul E. Peterson and Martin R. West, eds., *No Child Left Behind? The Politics and Practice of School Accountability* (Washington, DC: Brookings Institution Press, 2003).

80. Terry M. Moe, "Politics, Control, and the Future of School Accountability," in Paul E. Peterson and Martin R. West, eds., *No Child Left Behind? The Politics and Practice of School Accountability* (Washington, DC: Brookings Institution Press, 2003).

81. For exceptions, see Frederick M. Hess and Chester E. Finn Jr., eds., *Leaving No Child Behind? Options for Kids in Failing Schools* (New York: Palgrave Macmillan, 2004); Deborah Meier and George Wood, eds., *Many Children Left Behind*

(Boston: Beacon, 2004); Paul E. Peterson and Martin R. West, eds., *No Child Left Behind? The Politics and Practice of School Accountability* (Washington, DC: Brookings Institution Press, 2003).

2. The Problem of Quality

1. Throughout this book, unless the gender of a specific individual is known and noted, I refer to a student as "she," a teacher as "he," a principal as "she," and an administrative superior as "he."

2. National Association of Elementary School Principals and National Association of Secondary School Principals, *K–12 Principals Guide to No Child Left Behind*, 2–3.

3. James S. Coleman et al., *Equality of Educational Opportunity* (Washington, DC: U.S. Government Printing Office, 1966), 21–22.

4. Hochschild, "Rethinking Accountability Politics."

5. Sunderman and Kim, *Inspiring Vision, Disappointing Results,* 3.

6. Mancur Olson, *The Logic of Collective Action: Public Goods and the Theory of Groups* (Cambridge, MA: Harvard University Press, 1971).

7. Edward P. Lazear, "Educational Production," *Quarterly Journal of Economics* 116, no. 3 (2001).

8. Caroline Minter Hoxby, "How Teachers' Unions Affect Educational Production," *Quarterly Journal of Economics* 111, no. 3 (1996).

9. Dennis Epple and Richard E. Romano, "Competition between Private and Public Schools, Vouchers and Peer Group Effects,"*American Economic Review* 88, no. 1 (1998).

10. Lazear, "Educational Production."

11. Lazear, "Educational Production." Though in practice class size is much more complicated: individual schools cannot set their own budgets, and principals might choose different class sizes if they could.

12. Ronald Edmonds, "Effective Schools for the Urban Poor," *Educational Leadership* 37, no. 1 (1979): 21.

13. Ibid., 22.

14. See Harvey Averch et al., *How Effective is Schooling?* (Santa Monica, CA: Rand Corporation, 1972); Samuel Bowles and Henry Levin, "The Determinants of Scholastic Achievement—An Appraisal of Some Recent Evidence," *Journal of Human Resources* 3, no. 1 (1968); Wilber. B. Brookover and L. W. Lezotte, *Changes in School Characteristics Coincident with Changes in Student Achievement* (East Lansing: Michigan State University, College of Urban Development, 1977); Murnane, *The Impact of School Resources on the Learning of Inner City Children;* G. Weber, *Inner-City Children Can Be Taught to Read: Four Successful Schools* (Washington, DC: Council for Basic Education, 1971).

15. See also U.S. General Accounting Office, *Effective Schools Programs: Their Extent and Characteristics* (Washington, DC: U.S. General Accounting Office, 1989). For analyses of the effects of school principals on student achievement, see Dominic J. Brewer, "Principals and Student Outcomes: Evidence from U.S.

High Schools," *Economics of Education Review* 12, no. 4 (1993); Randall W. Eberts and Joe A. Stone, "Student Achievement in Public Schools: Do Principals Make a Difference?" *Economics of Education Review* 7, no. 3 (1988).

16. See Wilbur B. Brookover et al., *Elementary Social Environment and School Achievement* (East Lansing: Michigan State University, College of Urban Development, 1973); Wilbur B. Brookover, et al., *School Social Systems and Student Achievement* (New York: Praeger 1979); Anthony S. Bryk and Barbara Schneider, *Trust in Schools: A Core Resource for Development* (New York: Russell Sage Foundation, 2002).

17. Jonathan D. Jansen, "Effective Schools?" *Comparative Education* 31, no. 2 (1995); Brian Rowan, Steven T. Bossert, and David C. Dwyer, "Research on Effective Schools: A Cautionary Note," *Educational Researcher* 12, no. 4 (1983); John F. Witte and Daniel J. Walsh, "A Systematic Test of the Effective Schools Model," *Educational Evaluation and Policy Analysis* 12, no. 2 (1990).

18. This table is based on the analyses of Eric A. Hanushek, *Education and Race* (Lexington, MA: D.C. Heath, 1972); idem, "Conceptual and Empirical Issues in the Estimation of Educational Production Functions," *Journal of Human Resources* 14 no. 3 (1979); and Anita A. Summers and Barbara L. Wolfe, "Do Schools Make a Difference?" *American Economic Review* 67, no. 4 (1977).

19. Hanushek, "Conceptual and Empirical Issues in the Estimation of Educational Production Functions"; see also David H. Monk, "The Educational Production Function: Its Evolving Role in Policy Analysis," *Educational Evaluation and Policy Analysis* 11, no. 1 (1989).

20. See Hanushek and Raymond, "Lessons about the Designs of State Accountability Systems."

21. See David Card and Alan B. Krueger, "School Resources and Student Outcomes: An Overview of the Literature and New Evidence from North and South Carolina," *Journal of Economic Perspectives* 10, no. 4 (1996); Eric A. Hanushek, "Throwing Money at Schools," *Journal of Policy Analysis and Management* 1, no. 19 (1986); idem, "The Failure of Input-Based Schooling Policies," *Economic Journal* 113, no. 485 (2003); Hoxby, "How Teachers' Unions Affect Educational Production."

22. For a discussion of agency in relation to NCLB, see Terry M. Moe, "Politics, Control, and the Future of School Accountability," in Paul E. Peterson and Martin R. West, eds., *No Child Left Behind? The Politics and Practice of School Accountability* (Washington, DC: Brookings Institution Press, 2003).

23. School principals can be principals in this sense when teachers are the agents; school principals can also be agents when parents or school board members are the principals. I realize that this is more than a little confusing.

24. Moe, "Politics, Control, and the Future of School Accountability."

25. See Armen A. Alchian and Harold Demsetz, "Production, Information Costs, and Economic Organization," *American Economic Review* 62, no. 5 (1972); John Brehm and Scott Gates, *Working, Shirking, and Sabotage: Bureaucratic Response to a Democratic Public* (Ann Arbor: University of Michigan Press, 1997).

26. Of course, monitoring brings up the challenge of "who will monitor the monitor?" (Alchian and Demsetz, "Production, Information Costs, and Eco-

nomic Organization," 782). There is also the related challenge of 'adverse selection,' whereby agents' abilities are unknown, resulting in firms ending up with workers who are low-ability or unmotivated, given the offered wage or reward. Moe discusses this issue in relation to accountability and education ("Politics, Control, and the Future of School Accountability," 84–85). The problem with these economic models is that they are based on the assumption that individuals always prefer slacking off to working, failing to consider the possibility that some individuals go into education for more altruistic reasons or why some individuals go 'above and beyond' the call of duty.

27. Alchian and Demsetz, "Production, Information Costs, and Economic Organization."

28. Hanushek and Raymond discuss the implications of various test models for accountability and control. I will return to this topic in chapter 5 ("Lessons about the Designs of State Accountability Systems"); Moe identifies the problems of control and agency that will likely blunt the beneficial effects of any top-down accountability policy ("Politics, Control, and the Future of School Accountability").

29. James Q. Wilson, *Bureaucracy: What Government Agencies Do and Why They Do It* (New York: Basic Books, 1989).

30. Wilson asserts that his conception of coping organizations does not constitute a theory (*Bureaucracy*, 364). I disagree.

31. Wilson, *Bureaucracy*, 171.

32. Ibid., 175.

33. John E. Chubb and Terry M. Moe, *Politics, Markets, and America's Schools* (Washington, DC: Brookings Institution Press, 1990); Wilson, *Bureaucracy*.

34. John Dewey, *Experience and Education* (New York: Collier Books, 1938), 17.

35. Ibid., 25.

36. Wilson writes, "People matter, but organization matters also, and tasks matter most of all" (*Bureaucracy*, 173).

3. Making the Grade (or Not)

1. Tim Pugmire, "School Report Cards Out; Available Online," Minnesota Public Radio, 21 August 2003.

2. National Association of Elementary School Principals and National Association of Secondary School Principals, *K–12 Principals Guide to No Child Left Behind*, 16.

3. Education Minnesota, "Most Schools Get Three Stars" (press release), 2 September 2003.

4. The chapter subhead refers to V. O. Key Jr.'s foundational work, *Southern Politics in State and Nation* (New York: Vintage Books, 1949).

5. The Education Commission of the States maintains a comprehensive database on state policies and actions associated with No Child Left Behind (http://www.ecs.org).

6. The Education Commission of the States gave Minnesota a "Y" (its high-

est score, indicating that the state "appears on track") in all eleven of its categories of compliance in developing and implementing standards-based assessments ("NCLB Standards and Assessments: Minnesota," 2004).

7. This research was made possible through a Faculty Interactive Research Program grant from the Center for Urban and Regional Affairs at the University of Minnesota and took place in association with the University's Minnesota Center for Survey Research. It was also supported through a McKnight Summer Fellowship made possible through the Office of the Dean of the Graduate School of the University and a semester of leave awarded by the College of Liberal Arts at the University of Minnesota. Portions of this chapter were previously published as Scott Franklin Abernathy, "Evaluating the Impact of No Child Left Behind in Minnesota," *CURA Reporter* 36, no. 1 (2006).

8. When an individual principal was responsible for more than one school, a survey was sent to only one of the schools. The response rate was very high, at slightly less than 70 percent. Among charter school principals, the response rate dropped to 53 percent, probably at least partly because charter schools are more likely to have one principal overseeing separate "schools" within the same building, as well as the fact that many Minnesota charter schools are run by teams. I matched the survey results with extensive state data on student and school characteristics, achievement test scores, and status under No Child Left Behind in 2003 and 2004.

9. I e-mailed 126 regular and charter public school principals and received 28 replies. I asked nine questions:

1. What effect do you think No Child Left Behind is having on your leadership at this school?
2. How much time do you spend ensuring that your school makes adequate yearly progress?
3. Have these efforts changed how you allocate your time as principal in other areas? If so, how?
4. What effect is No Child Left Behind having on the performance of your teachers?
5. Is it affecting how your teachers choose to allocate their time? If so, how?
6. What aspects of your leadership are not captured in the testing associated with No Child Left Behind?
7. Is there a better way to measure these aspects of your leadership?
8. What effect do you think No Child Left Behind will have on the achievement of your students? How so?
9. Do you have any other thoughts about No Child Left Behind and your leadership?

10. Robert Putnam, *Bowling Alone: The Collapse and Revival of American Community* (New York: Simon and Schuster, 2000). My thanks to R. Douglas Arnold for clarification of this point.

11. Minnesota Office of Educational Accountability and the University of Minnesota College of Education and Human Development, "The Minnesota Basic Skills Test: Performance Gaps on the Reading and Mathematics Tests from 1996 to 2001, by Gender, Ethnicity, Limited English Proficiency, Individual Education Plans, and Socio-Economic Status."

12. Minnesota Department of Education, "No Questions Left Behind: A Comprehensive Guide to Minnesota's Accountability Plan under the No Child Left Behind Act" (2004), 1.

13. Minnesota Department of Education, *NCLB Adequate Yearly Progress (AYP) System Requirements/Business Rules* (2003). Test days in Minnesota fall between January and March, depending on the grade and subject.

14. If, for example, a school had forty third-graders with limited English proficiency and thirty-seven, rather than thirty-eight, of these students took the test, then the school would fail to make AYP. One Minnesota elementary school failed to make AYP because only fifty-nine of sixty-three students eligible for free or reduced-price lunch took the 2002 test. Though an administrative error occurred (a sixtieth student showed up but was not counted), the school remained on the list of those schools failing to make AYP because it failed to file an appeal to the state within thirty days (Britt Robson, "Built to Fail," *City Pages,* 10 March 2004). There are proposals to exempt specific students for medical and other reasons, on a case-by-case basis, or in the case of students with irregular attendance patterns (National School Boards Association, "NSBA's Bill to Improve No Child Left Behind").

15. Minnesota Department of Education, "No Questions Left Behind."

16. Norman Draper, "Lofty Goals May Leave Schools Far Behind," *Minneapolis Star Tribune,* 15 December 2002.

17. Minnesota Office of the Legislative Auditor, *Evaluation Report: No Child Left Behind,* xi.

18. Ibid., 26.

19. Herbert A. Simon, *Administrative Behavior* (New York: Free Press, 1945).

20. Tim Pugmire, "List of Underachieving Schools Shrinks to 144," Minnesota Public Radio, 14 August 2003.

21. Steve Brandt, "Homework for the Holidays," *Minneapolis Star Tribune,* 18 December 2004.

22. Dan Wascoe, "Take Your Children to Work . . . Later," *Minneapolis Star Tribune,* 16 April 2005.

23. Minnesota Office of the Legislative Auditor, *Evaluation Report: No Child Left Behind* (summary letter).

24. Ibid., 29.

25. Draper, "Lofty Goals May Leave Schools Far Behind."

26. Novak and Fuller, *Penalizing Diverse Schools?* 5.

27. Ibid., 1.

28. Center on Education Policy, *From the Capital to the Classroom,* 1.

29. Minnesota Department of Education, "Governor Pawlenty: Minnesota's Schools Get Even Better" (press release), 29 August 2005.

30. George Wood finds a very similar pattern in Ohio's "Blue ribbon"

schools ("A View From the Field: NCLB's Effects on Classrooms and Schools," in Deborah Meier and George Wood, eds., *Many Children Left Behind: How the No Child Left Behind Act Is Damaging Our Children and Our Schools* [Boston: Beacon, 2004]). Researchers have found similar patterns in the negative relationship between percentage of Latino students and classification as "exemplary" in Texas's public schools (Kane and Staiger, "Unintended Consequences of Racial Subgroup Rules," 162).

31. The correlation coefficient is 0.78.

32. Center on Education Policy, *From the Capital to the Classroom.*

33. Chubb and Moe, *Politics, Markets, and America's Schools.*

34. Out of concern over potential problems of nondifferentiation and lack of a linear scale in the time-spent variable, I constructed the following alternative scorings of the variables: having spent a great deal of time on each area and the points awarded to one activity divided by the total number of points awarded on all seven questions (in separate regressions). In all cases, the substantive conclusions remain unchanged; in fact, standard errors were significantly smaller when relative variables were looked at individually. Nevertheless, I chose to present the more straightforward data. In any case, my results are quite robust.

35. One regret about these data is that I do not have a reliable measure of actual class size. Though I could simply divide number of students by number of teachers, it would produce a noisy statistic.

36. Gary King, Michael Tomz, and Jason Wittenberg, "Making the Most of Statistical Analysis: Improving Interpretation and Presentation," *American Journal of Political Science* 44, no. 2 (2000). Full results of the probit regression model are presented in the appendix.

37. I also constructed a similar set of models using a school's status as newly identified as having failed to make AYP as the dependent variable. The substantive conclusions remain unchanged; in fact, standard errors on the key time-allocation variables were somewhat smaller.

38. Eberts and Stone, "Student Achievement in Public Schools"; Jane Hannaway, "The Organization and Management of Public and Catholic Schools: Looking Inside the 'Black Box,'" *International Journal of Educational Research* 15, no. 5 (1991).

39. For a discussion on the relationship between political activism and resource inequalities, see Sidney Verba, Kay Lehman Schlozman, and Henry E. Brady, *Voice and Equality: Civic Volunteerism in American Politics* (Cambridge, MA: Harvard University Press, 1995).

40. Walter Murphy, *Elements of Judicial Strategy* (Chicago: University of Chicago Press, 1964), 208. Murphy is discussing the work of Stanley Kelley ("The Presidential Campaign," in Paul T. David, ed., *The Presidential Election and Transition 1960–61* [Washington, DC: Brookings Institution Press, 1961]).

4. Top-Down and Bottom Up

1. Scott Franklin Abernathy, *School Choice and the Future of American Democracy* (Ann Arbor: University of Michigan Press, 2005).

2. Chubb and Moe, *Politics, Markets, and America's Schools.*

3. Krista Kafer, "No Child Left Behind: Where Do We Go From Here?" *Heritage Foundation Backgrounder,* no. 1775 (2004).

4. Tom Loveless discusses the problem of measuring achievement in charter schools, and suggests that new charters receive a two-year grace period before being subject to NCLB's sanctions. He does not, however, empirically explore NCLB's impact on charter schools ("Charter School Achievement and Accountability," in Paul E. Peterson and Martin R. West, eds., *No Child Left Behind? The Politics and Practice of School Accountability* [Washington, DC: Brookings Institution Press, 2003]).

5. Gary Miron and Christopher Nelson, *Student Academic Achievement in Charter Schools: What We Know and Why We Know So Little,* Occasional Paper 41 (New York: National Center for the Study of Privatization in Education, Teachers College, Columbia University, 2001)

6. Chester E. Finn Jr., Bruno V. Manno, and Greg Vanourek, *Charter Schools in Action: Renewing Public Education* (Princeton: Princeton University Press, 2000).

7. Gregg Vanourek, *State of the Charter Movement 2005* (Washington, DC: The Charter School Leadership Council, 2005), 5.

8. Ibid., 7.

9. Ibid., 11.

10. Minnesota Department of Education, "No Questions Left Behind."

11. Moe, "Politics, Control, and the Future of School Accountability," 102. For a thorough treatment of market-based and accountability-based incentives, see Harris and Herington, "Accountability, Standards, and the Growing Achievement Gap."

12. Chester E. Finn Jr., "Making School Reform Work," *Public Interest* 148 (summer 2002), 94.

13. Loveless, "Charter School Achievement and Accountability," 184.

14. Brehm and Gates, *Working, Shirking, and Sabotage.*

15. Researchers have commented on the possibility that some people choose to go into education simply because they are lazy and know that, given the informational challenges to measuring their quality (combined with tenure), education is the place for them. Economists call this problem one of "adverse selection" (Moe, "Politics, Control, and the Future of School Accountability"). More evidence of its prevalence in education, or lack thereof, is probably needed. Moe's framing of the challenges of No Child Left Behind in terms of agency, however, is in one of the most promising approaches for predicting the legislation's outcomes.

16. Simon, *Administrative Behavior.*

17. Canice Prendergast, "The Provision of Incentives in Firms," *Journal of Economic Literature* 37, no. 1 (1999), 8.

18. Steve Farkas, Jean Johnson, and Ann Duffett, "Rolling Up Their Sleeves: Superintendents and Principals Talk about What's Needed to Fix Public Schools" (New York: Public Agenda, 2003).

19. The response rates that Farkas, Johnson, and Duffet obtained—34 percent for superintendents and 23 percent for principals—were quite a bit lower

than what I observed in the Minnesota Schools Survey but still remained in line with typical response rates for these surveys.

20. Farkas, Johnson, and Duffett, "Rolling Up Their Sleeves," 53.

21. Ibid., 63.

22. Ibid., 64.

23. Ibid., 56.

24. I am grateful to Paul Manna for clarification of this point.

25. Emphases are the principal's.

26. To examine the possibility that a principal's patterns of leadership might be related to the fact that charter schools attract different kinds of leaders, I conducted Hausman tests of the results of two-stage least squares estimation for each of the models in this chapter, to see if the use of instrumented variables would be appropriate (I used ordinary least squares for the five-point scales for the comparison, as two-stage least squares estimation with ordered probit regression is extremely complicated and beyond my programming ability). I used principals' demographic characteristics as my instruments. None of the differences between the instrumented and noninstrumented regressions for the results in figure 11 were significant. In the two-stage least squares estimation for the results in figure 12, the standard errors on the charter school dummy variables were considerably larger; however, I was again unable to reject the null hypothesis of no systematic differences between the coefficient estimates. The standard errors on the charter school variables associated with figure 13 were actually smaller; however, the differences were not statistically significant. Finally, the alternate models of figure 14 did not have enough predictive power to give me confidence in their estimates; however, the coefficient estimates on the charter school dummy variables were of the same direction and significance as in the base (ordinary least squares) models.

27. I was not inclined to include something like membership in a minority group in my models as I had no theoretical basis for arguing precisely why or how this information should matter. Out of a concern for the underlying methodological issues, however, I did so in this chapter.

28. See Abernathy, *School Choice and the Future of American Democracy*. These models also included the expected effect of NCLB on principals' influence, to capture any inherent optimism or pessimism about the law's effects.

29. The reference cells in all of the regressions are principals of regular public schools that made AYP.

30. Regrettably, these data do not include a separate question for district superintendents. This question was omitted because it would not have made much sense in the case of charter schools, it would have been useful to ask the question of regular public school principals only.

31. Chubb and Moe, *Politics, Markets, and America's Schools*.

32. Only the coefficient estimate on the teacher variable was statistically significant for charter schools.

33. The underlying regressions used the same five-point time used in the survey. The simulations present the predicted probabilities that a principal would

respond that a "great deal of time" was spent on the activity (that is, a five on the scale).

34. My thanks to Andrew Rotherham and Jeffrey Henig for clarification of this point.

5. Rethinking Assessment

1. Hanushek and Raymond, "Lessons about the Designs of State Accountability Systems," 130–31.

2. Robert H. Meyer, "Value-Added Indicators of School Performance: A Primer," *Economics of Education Review* 16, no. 3 (1997).

3. Hanushek and Raymond refer to these as "status change" models ("Lessons about the Designs of State Accountability Systems," 131).

4. Kane and Staiger, "Unintended Consequences of Racial Subgroup Rules," 153.

5. Loveless, "Charter School Achievement and Accountability," 191.

6. Hanushek and Raymond, "Lessons about the Designs of State Accountability Systems," 133.

7. U.S. Department of Education, "Secretary Spellings Announces Growth Model Pilot, Addresses Chief State School Officers' Annual Policy Forum in Richmond" (press release), 18 November 2005.

8. National Education Association, "U.S. Education Department Validates NEA's Concerns, Proposes More Flexibility under 'No Child Left Behind'" (press release), 18 November 2005.

9. Jane Hannaway and Kendra Bishoff, "Florida: Confusions, Constraints, and Cascading Scenarios," in Frederick M. Hess and Chester E. Finn Jr., eds., *Leaving No Child Behind? Options for Kids in Failing Schools* (New York: Palgrave Macmillan, 2004), 98.

10. Only grade three and grade five tests were used in both 2003 and 2004 for NCLB compliance in Minnesota. The pattern of results of the grade five tests is the same.

11. Kane and Staiger, "Unintended Consequences of Racial Subgroup Rules," 164.

12. Meyer, "Value-Added Indicators of School Performance."

13. Herdman, Smith, and Doran, "Value-Added Analysis," 2.

14. William L. Sanders and Sandra P. Horn, "Research Findings from the Tennessee Value-Added Assessment System (TVAAS) Database: Implications for Educational Evaluation and Research," *Journal of Personnel Evaluation in Education* 12, no. 3 (1998), 1.

15. Robert H. Meyer, "Value-Added Indicators: Do They Make a Difference? Evidence From the Milwaukee Public Schools," paper presented at the annual meeting of the American Educational Research Association, New Orleans, 2002.

16. Helen Ladd and Randall P. Walsh, "Implementing Value-Added Measures of School Effectiveness: Getting the Incentives Right," *Economics of Education Review* 21, no. 1 (2001).

17. Yeow Meng Thum, *No Child Left Behind: Methodological Challenges and Recommendations for Measuring Adequate Yearly Progress* (Los Angeles: Center for the Study of Evaluation, National Center for Research on Evaluation, Standards, and Student Testing, Graduate School of Education and Information Studies, University of California, Los Angeles, 2003).

18. Ladd and Walsh, "Implementing Value-Added Measures of School Effectiveness."

19. Darrel Drury and Harold Duran, "The Value of Value-Added Analysis," *National School Boards Association Policy Brief* 3, no. 1 (2003).

20. Ladd and Walsh, "Implementing Value-Added Measures of School Effectiveness."

21. Mark L. Davison and Leslie J. Davison, "Growth and Value-Added Issues in Minnesota," paper presented at the conference of the Council of Chief State School Officers (CCSSO) on the Use of Growth Models Based on Student-Level Data in School Accountability, Washington, DC, 2004.

22. Minnesota Office of the Legislative Auditor, *Evaluation Report: No Child Left Behind,* 51.

23. Minnesota Department of Education, "Governor Pawlenty Announces 'Value-Added' Growth Model to Measure Individual Student Progress" (press release), 13 October 2004.

24. Minnesota Statute 120B.30(c)(2).

25. John Brehm and Wendy Rahn, "Individual-Level Evidence for the Causes and Consequences of Social Capital," *American Journal of Political Science* 41, no. 3 (1997); Bryk and Schneider, *Trust in Schools;* James S. Coleman, "Social Capital in the Creation of Human Capital," *American Journal of Sociology* 94 (Supplement), (1988); Robert Putnam, *Making Democracy Work: Civic Traditions in Modern Italy* (Princeton: Princeton University Press, 1993); idem, "Bowling Alone: America's Declining Social Capital," *Journal of Democracy* 6, no. 1 (1995).

26. Andrew C. Porter, "Creating a System of School Process Indicators," *Educational Evaluation and Policy Analysis* 13, no. 1 (1991), 13; Porter argues that process "indicators should not be used for accountability purposes" (24). I disagree, but note that the incorporation of parent and student satisfaction surveys is a different and broader approach that that which Porter discusses. Jeannie Oakes calls these "context indicators" ("What Educational Indicators? The Case for Assessing the School Context," *Educational Evaluation and Policy Analysis* 11, no. 2 [1989], 181).

27. John J. DiIulio Jr., "Rethinking the Criminal Justice System: Toward a New Paradigm," in *Performance Measures for the Criminal Justice System* (Washington, DC: U.S Department of Justice, Office of Justice Programs, Bureau of Justice Statistics, 1993), 4.

28. George L. Kelling, *"Broken Windows" and Police Discretion* (Washington, DC: U.S. Department of Justice, Office of Justice Programs, 1999).

29. I use the term *production model* rather than *performance model* or *process model,* which would be more consistent with the use of process indicators. In education, performance is such a heavily laden term that I avoid using it in this con-

text, and *production* seems to better capture the constructed nature of educational quality. For a discussion on the possibility of using measures such as school climate and parental satisfaction in schools, though in a secondary role to the use of student test outcome measures, see McAdams et al., *Urban School District Accountability Systems* (Denver: Education Commission of the States and the Center for Reform of School Systems, 2003).

30. Charles H. Logan, "Criminal Justice Performance: Measures for Prisons," in *Performance Measures for the Criminal Justice System* (Washington, DC: U.S Department of Justice, Office of Justice Programs, Bureau of Justice Statistics, 1993).

31. DiIulio, "Rethinking the Criminal Justice System," 5.

32. John J. DiIulio Jr., "Measuring Performance When There Is No Bottom Line," in *Performance Measures for the Criminal Justice System* (Washington, DC: U.S Department of Justice, Office of Justice Programs, Bureau of Justice Statistics, 1993), 154.

33. James Q. Wilson, "The Problem of Defining Agency Success," in *Performance Measures for the Criminal Justice System* (Washington, DC: U.S Department of Justice, Office of Justice Programs, Bureau of Justice Statistics, 1993), 163.

34. Jeannie Oakes's analysis appears to concur with the idea of experiential organizations: "Educators, parents, and policy makers also worry about the quality of *experiences* that children have in school. Consequently, indicator systems should also include measures of these experiences" ("What Educational Indicators?" [1989], 182). Italics are the author's.

35. Minneapolis Public Schools, "School Information Report," 2004. Response rates for the student portion of the surveys used in this analysis were 81 percent for K–8 schools and 90 percent for K–6 schools. Response rates for staff were 68 percent for K–8 schools and 76 percent ·for K–6 schools. Separate response rates for teachers were not available. In these analyses, I focus only on students and teachers, as teachers are included in overall staff results and are more central to my analysis. Though publicly available, these data are used with the verbal permission of the Minneapolis Public Schools.

36. As Wilson (*Bureaucracy*) has observed, however, and as I have shown, measuring outcomes in organizations like schools is a fundamentally difficult undertaking.

37. The first two indicators were framed in the affirmative, as in percentages of students and teachers who were being kept from their tasks. For the variable, I simply used one hundred minus the school score to align all of the variables along the same continuum (Minneapolis Public Schools, "School Information Report").

38. Abernathy, *School Choice and the Future of American Democracy;* Mark Schneider et al., "Networks to Nowhere: Segregation and Stratification in Networks of Information about Schools," *American Journal of Political Science* 41, no. 4 (1997); Clarence N. Stone et al., *Building Civic Capacity: The Politics of Reforming Urban Schools* (Lawrence: University Press of Kansas, 2001); Verba, Schlozman, and Brady, *Voice and Equality.*

39. The confidence intervals on these predicted probabilities were quite large, which is unsurprising given the small number of schools in the data. The coefficient estimates on these differences were significant in the underlying regressions, though I caution that these simulations illustrate the impact of differences in leadership rather than to prove specific point values.

6. Carrots, Sticks, and Unbroken Windows

1. Sunderman and Kim, *Inspiring Vision, Disappointing Results,* 9.

2. The term *middle-out,* at least as it relates to educational reform, appears to have been first used by Kate Malloy in a study of New York City District 2: "Overall, the listening and communicating that occur throughout the district are meant to produce not only a balance between top-down and bottom-up influences, but a powerful 'middle-out' component, a sort of clearing house of substantive and strategic information processed through the role of the principal" (*Building a Learning Community: The Story of New York City Community School District #2* [Pittsburgh: University of Pittsburgh, Learning Research and Development Center, 1998], 6); see also Lauren B. Resnick and Megan Williams Hall, "Learning Organizations for Sustainable Education Reform," *Daedalus* 127, no. 4 (1998).

3. See Jeffrey Henig, *Rethinking School Choice: Limits of the Market Metaphor* (Princeton: Princeton University Press, 1994).

4. Stone et al., *Building Civic Capacity.*

5. Loveless, "Charter School Achievement and Accountability," 191.

6. No Child Left Behind authorizes the National Center for Education Statistics to incorporate "anonymous student surveys and anonymous teacher surveys" in assessing the prevalence of "illegal drug use and violence" (20 U.S.C. § 7132).

7. David P. Ericson and Frederick S. Ellett Jr., "The Question of the Student in Educational Reform," *Education Policy Analysis Archives* 10, no. 31 (2002).

8. Mary Ann Lachat, *Data-Driven High School Reform: The Breaking Ranks Model* (Providence, RI: Brown University, 2001), 11.

9. Lachat, *Data-Driven High School Reform,* 13; See also Linda Darling-Hammond, "Reframing the School Reform Agenda," *Phi Delta Kappan* 74, no. 10 (1993).

10. See, for example, Packer, "No Child Left Behind and Academic Yearly Progress—Fundamental Flaws."

11. Harris and Herrington discuss this issue broadly in the context of a comparative study of educational reform in the United States but not specifically related to No Child Left Behind ("Accountability, Standards, and the Growing Achievement Gap").

12. Bob Chase, "Making a Difference," in Joshua Cohen and Joel Rogers, eds., *Will Standards Save Public Education?* (Boston: Beacon, 2000), 41–42.

13. Minnesota Office of the Legislative Auditor, *Evaluation Report: No Child Left Behind,* 25.

14. Council of the Great City Schools, *Foundations for Success in the Minneapolis Public Schools* (Washington, DC: Council of the Great City Schools, 2004), 9.

15. McAdams et al., *Urban School District Accountability Systems*, 15.

16. This suggestion would necessitate the resolution of some important financial issues. If districts are forced to leave staff in some schools in place in the presence of budget cuts, then they would be saddled with an additional financial burden if not reimbursed for these extra costs by the federal government.

References

Abernathy, Scott Franklin. 2005. *School Choice and the Future of American Democracy.* Ann Arbor: University of Michigan Press.

———. 2006. "Evaluating the Impact of No Child Left Behind in Minnesota." *Center for Urban and Regional Affairs Reporter* 36 (1): 17–23. Available at www.cura.umn.edu.

Alchian, Armen A., and Harold Demsetz. 1972. "Production, Information Costs, and Economic Organization." *American Economic Review* 62 (5): 777–95.

Antle, W. James, III. 2005. "The Bull That Never Ends." *American Conservative,* August 1.

Archibald, George. 2005. "Utah Set to Reject No Child Left Behind." *Washington Times,* February 23.

Averch, Harvey, Stephen J. Carroll, Theodore S. Donaldson, Herbert J. Kiesling, and John Pincus. 1972. *How Effective Is Schooling?* Santa Monica, CA: Rand.

Barton, Paul E. 2003. *Parsing the Achievement Gap.* Princeton, NJ: Educational Testing Service, Policy Information Center.

Betts, Julian R., and Anne Danenberg. 2003. "The Effects of Accountability in California." In *No Child Left Behind? The Politics and Practice of School Accountability,* edited by Paul E. Peterson and Martin R. West. Washington, DC: Brookings Institution Press.

Betts, Julian R., Andrew C. Zau, and Lorien A. Rice. 2003. *Determinants of Student Achievement: New Evidence from San Diego.* San Francisco: Public Policy Institute of California.

Bowles, Samuel, and Henry M. Levin. 1968. "The Determinants of Scholastic Achievement—An Appraisal of Some Recent Evidence." *Journal of Human Resources* 3 (1): 3–24.

Brandt, Steve. 2004. "Homework for the Holidays." *Minneapolis Star Tribune,* December 18.

Brehm, John, and Scott Gates. 1997. *Working, Shirking, and Sabotage: Bureaucratic Response to a Democratic Public.* Ann Arbor: University of Michigan Press.

Brehm, John, and Wendy Rahn. 1997. "Individual-Level Evidence for the Causes and Consequences of Social Capital." *American Journal of Political Science* 41 (3): 999–1023.

Brewer, Dominic J. 1993. "Principals and Student Outcomes: Evidence from U.S. High Schools." *Economics of Education Review* 12 (4): 281–92.

Brookover, Wilbur B., Charles Beady, Patricia Flood, John Schweitzer, and Joe Wisenbaker. 1979. *School Social Systems and Student Achievement.* New York: Praeger.

Brookover, Wilbur B., Richard J. Gigliotti, Ronald D. Henderson, and Jeffrey M. Schneider. 1973. *Elementary School Social Environment and School Achievement.* East Lansing: Michigan State University, College of Urban Development.

Brookover, Wilbur B., and L. W. Lezotte. 1977. *Changes in School Characteristics Coincident with Changes in Student Achievement.* East Lansing: Michigan State University, College of Urban Development.

Bryk, Anthony S., and Barbara Schneider. 2002. *Trust in Schools: A Core Resource for Development.* New York: Russell Sage Foundation.

Card, David, and Alan B. Krueger. 1996. "School Resources and Student Outcomes: An Overview of the Literature and New Evidence from North and South Carolina." *Journal of Economic Perspectives* 10 (4): 31–50.

Casserly, Michael. 2004. "Choice and Supplemental Services in America's Great City Schools." In *Leaving No Child Behind? Options for Kids in Failing Schools,* edited by Frederick M. Hess and Chester E. Finn Jr. New York: Palgrave Macmillan.

Center on Education Policy. 2004. *Rule Changes Could Help More Schools Meet Test Score Targets for the No Child Left Behind Act.* Washington, DC: Center on Education Policy.

———. 2005. *From the Capital to the Classroom: Year 3 of the No Child Left Behind Act.* Washington, DC: Center on Education Policy.

Chase, Bob. 2000. "Making a Difference." In *Will Standards Save Public Education?* edited by Joshua Cohen and Joel Rogers. Boston: Beacon.

Chubb, John E., and Terry M. Moe. 1990. *Politics, Markets, and America's Schools.* Washington, DC: Brookings Institution Press.

Coleman, James S. 1988. "Social Capital in the Creation of Human Capital." *American Journal of Sociology* 94 (Supplement): S95–120.

Coleman, James S., E. Q. Campbell, C. J. Hobson, J. McPortland, A. M. Mood, F. D. Weinfield, and R. L. York. 1966. *Equality of Educational Opportunity.* Washington, DC: U.S. Government Printing Office.

Council of the Great City Schools. 2004. *Foundations for Success in the Minneapolis Public Schools.* Washington, DC: Council of the Great City Schools.

Cronin, John, G. Gage Kingsbury, Martha S. McCall, and Branin Bowe. 2005. "The Impact of the No Child Left Behind Act on Student Achievement and Growth: 2005 Edition." Lake Oswego, OR: Northwest Evaluation Association.

Darling-Hammond, Linda. 1993. "Reframing the School Reform Agenda." *Phi Delta Kappan* 74 (10): 752–61.

————. 2004. "From 'Separate but Equal' to 'No Child Left Behind': The Collision of New Standards and Old Inequalities." In *Many Children Left Behind: How the No Child Left Behind Act Is Damaging Our Children and Our Schools,* edited by Deborah Meier and George Wood. Boston: Beacon.

Davison, Mark L., and Leslie J. Davison. 2004. "Growth and Value-Added Issues in Minnesota." Paper presented at the conference of the Council of Chief State School Officers on the Use of Growth Models Based on Student-Level Data in School Accountability, Washington, DC, November 15–16.

Dewey, John. 1938. *Experience and Education.* New York: Collier.

DiIulio, John J., Jr. 1993a. "Measuring Performance When There Is No Bottom Line." In *Performance Measures for the Criminal Justice System.* Washington, DC: U.S. Department of Justice, Office of Justice Programs, Bureau of Justice Statistics.

————. 1993b. "Rethinking the Criminal Justice System: Toward a New Paradigm." In *Performance Measures for the Criminal Justice System.* Washington, DC: U.S. Department of Justice, Office of Justice Programs, Bureau of Justice Statistics.

Draper, Norman. 2002. "Lofty Goals May Leave Schools Far Behind." *Minneapolis Star Tribune,* December 15.

Drury, Darrel, and Harold Duran. 2003. "The Value of Value-Added Analysis." *National School Boards Association Policy Brief* 3 (1): 1–4.

Eberts, Randall W., and Joe A. Stone. 1988. "Student Achievement in Public Schools: Do Principals Make a Difference?" *Economics of Education Review* 7 (3): 291–99.

Edmonds, Ronald. 1979. "Effective Schools for the Urban Poor." *Educational Leadership* 37 (1): 15–24.

Education Commission of the States. 2004a. "ECS Report to the Nation: State Implementation of the No Child Left Behind Act." Available at www.ecs.org.

————. 2004b. "NCLB Standards and Assessments: Minnesota." 2004. Available at www.ecs.org.

Education Minnesota. 2003. "Most Schools Get Three Stars" (press release). September 2.

Epple, Dennis, and Richard E. Romano. 1998. "Competition between Private and Public Schools, Vouchers, and Peer Group Effects." *American Economic Review* 88 (1): 33–62.

Ericson, David P., and Frederick S. Ellett Jr. 2002. "The Question of the Student in Educational Reform." *Education Policy Analysis Archives.* Available at http://epaa.asu.edu/v10n31/.

Farkas, Steve, Jean Johnson, and Ann Duffett. 2003. "Rolling Up Their Sleeves: Superintendents and Principals Talk about What's Needed to Fix Public Schools." Public Agenda. Available at www.publicagenda.org.

Finn, Chester E., Jr. 2002. "Making School Reform Work." *Public Interest* 148 (summer): 85–95.

Finn, Chester E., Jr., Bruno V. Manno, and Greg Vanourek. 2000. *Charter Schools in Action: Renewing Public Education.* Princeton: Princeton University Press.

"First National Suit over Education Law." 2005. *AP Newswire.* April 20.

Hannaway, Jane. 1991. "The Organization and Management of Public and Catholic Schools: Looking inside the 'Black Box.'" *International Journal of Educational Research* 15 (5): 463–81.

Hannaway, Jane, and Kendra Bishoff. 2004. "Florida: Confusions, Constraints, and Cascading Scenarios." In *Leaving No Child Behind? Options for Kids in Failing Schools,* edited by Frederick M. Hess and Chester E. Finn Jr. New York: Palgrave Macmillan.

Hanushek, Eric. A. 1972. *Education and Race.* Lexington, MA: Heath.

———. 1979. "Conceptual and Empirical Issues in the Estimation of Educational Production Functions." *Journal of Human Resources* 14 (3): 351–88.

———. 1986. "Throwing Money at Schools." *Journal of Policy Analysis and Management* 1 (19): 19–41.

———. 1996. "Measuring Investment in Education." *Journal of Economic Perspectives* 10 (4): 9–30.

———. 2003. "The Failure of Input-Based Schooling Policies." *Economic Journal* 113 (485): F64–98.

Hanushek, Eric A., and Margaret E. Raymond. 2003. "Lessons about the Designs of State Accountability Systems." In *No Child Left Behind? The Politics and Practice of School Accountability,* edited by Paul E. Peterson and Martin R. West. Washington, DC: Brookings Institution Press.

Harris, Douglas N., and Carolyn D. Herington. 2006. "Accountability, Standards, and the Growing Achievement Gap: Lessons from the Past Half-Century." *American Journal of Education* 111 (2): 209–38.

Henig, Jeffrey. 1994. *Rethinking School Choice: Limits of the Market Metaphor.* Princeton: Princeton University Press.

Herdman, Paul A., Nelson Smith, and Harold Doran. 2002. "Value-Added Analysis: A Critical Component of Determining Adequate Yearly Progress." *Charter School Friends Network Policy Brief.* Available at http://www.charterfriends.org/NCLB_ValueAdded.doc.

Hess, Frederick M. 2003. "Refining or Retreating? High-Stakes Accountability in the States." In *No Child Left Behind? The Politics and Practice of School Accountability,* edited by Paul E. Peterson and Martin R. West. Washington, DC: Brookings Institution Press.

Hess, Frederick M., and Chester E. Finn Jr., eds. 2004. *Leaving No Child Behind? Options for Kids in Failing Schools.* New York: Palgrave Macmillan.

Hochschild, Jennifer. 2003. "Rethinking Accountability Politics." In *No Child Left Behind? The Politics and Practice of School Accountability,* edited by Paul E. Peterson and Martin R. West. Washington, DC: Brookings Institution Press.

Hochschild, Jennifer L., and Nathan Scovronick. 2003. *The American Dream and the Public Schools.* New York: Oxford University Press.

Howell, William. 2004. "Fumbling for an Exit Key: Parents, Choice, and the Future of NCLB." In *Leaving No Child Behind? Options for Kids in Failing Schools,* edited by Frederick M. Hess and Chester E. Finn Jr. New York: Palgrave Macmillan.

Hoxby, Caroline Minter. 1996. "How Teachers' Unions Affect Educational Production." *Quarterly Journal of Economics* 111 (3): 671–718.

———. 2000. *Peer Effects in the Classroom: Learning from Gender and Race Variation.* Working Paper 7867. Cambridge, MA: National Bureau of Economic Research.

Jansen, Jonathan D. 1995. "Effective Schools?" *Comparative Education* 31 (2): 181–200.

Jencks, Christopher, et al. 1972. *Inequality: A Reassessment of the Effect of Family and Schooling in America.* New York: Basic Books.

Jennings, Jack. 2002. "Stricter Federal Demands, Bigger State Role: What to Expect from the No Child Left Behind Act." *State Education Standard* (spring). National Association of State Boards of Education. Available at www.nasbe.org.

Kafer, Krista. 2004. "No Child Left Behind: Where Do We Go from Here?" *Heritage Foundation Backgrounder* 1775 (July): 1–8.

Kane, Thomas J., and Douglas O. Staiger. 2003. "Unintended Consequences of Racial Subgroup Rules." In *No Child Left Behind? The Politics and Practice of School Accountability,* edited by Paul E. Peterson and Martin R. West. Washington, DC: Brookings Institution Press.

Kelley, Stanley. 1961. "The Presidential Campaign." In *The Presidential Election and Transition 1960–61,* edited by Paul T. David. Washington, DC: Brookings Institution Press.

Kelling, George L. 1999. *"Broken Windows" and Police Discretion.* Washington, DC: U.S. Department of Justice, Office of Justice Programs.

Key, V. O. 1949. *Southern Politics in State and Nation.* New York: Vintage Books.

King, Gary, Michael Tomz, and Jason Wittenberg. 2000. "Making the Most of Statistical Analysis: Improving Interpretation and Presentation." *American Journal of Political Science* 44 (2): 341–55.

Kohn, Alfie. 2000. *The Case against Standardized Testing: Raising the Scores, Ruining the Schools.* Portsmouth, NH: Heinemann.

———. 2004. "NCLB and the Effort to Privatize Public Education." In *Many Children Left Behind: How the No Child Left Behind Act Is Damaging Our Children and Our Schools,* edited by Deborah Meier and George Wood. Boston: Beacon.

Koretz, Daniel M. 2002. "Limitations in the Use of Achievement Tests as Measures of Educators' Productivity." *Journal of Human Resources* 37 (4): 752–77.

Lachat, Mary Ann. 2001. *Data-Driven High School Reform: The Breaking Ranks Model.* Providence, RI: Brown University.

Ladd, Helen, and Randall P. Walsh. 2002. "Implementing Value-Added Measures of School Effectiveness: Getting the Incentives Right." *Economics of Education Review* 21 (1): 1–17.

Lazear, Edward P. 2001. "Educational Production." *Quarterly Journal of Economics* 116 (3): 777–803.

Levitt, Steven D. 2005. *Freakonomics: A Rogue Economist Explores the Hidden Side of Everything.* New York: Morrow.

Linn, Robert L. 2004. "Rethinking the No Child Left Behind Accountability System." Paper presented at the Center on Education Policy Forum on Ideas to Improve the Accountability Provisions under the No Child Left Behind Act, Washington, DC, July 28.

Linn, Robert L., Eva L. Baker, and Damian W. Betebenner. 2002. "Accountability Systems: Implications of Requirements of the No Child Left Behind Act of 2001." *Educational Researcher* 31 (6): 3–6.

Linn, Robert L., Eva L. Baker, and Stephen B. Dunbar. 1991. "Complex, Performance-Based Assessment: Expectations and Validation Criteria." *Educational Researcher* 20 (8): 15–21.

Locy, Toni. 2005. "Judge Tosses Out NCLB Lawsuit." *Minneapolis Star Tribune,* November 23.

Logan, Charles H. 1993. "Criminal Justice Performance: Measures for Prisons." In *Performance Measures for the Criminal Justice System.* Washington, DC: U.S. Department of Justice, Office of Justice Programs, Bureau of Justice Statistics.

Loveless, Tom. 2003a. "Charter School Achievement and Accountability." In *No Child Left Behind? The Politics and Practice of School Accountability,* edited by Paul E. Peterson and Martin R. West. Washington, DC: Brookings Institution Press.

———. 2003b. "How Well Are American Students Learning?" In *Brown Center Report on American Education.* Washington, DC: Brookings Institution Press.

Lynn, Ronnie. 2005. "Utah Bucks Feds on Schools." *Salt Lake Tribune,* April 20.

Malloy, Kate. 1998. *Building a Learning Community: The Story of New York City Community School District #2.* Pittsburgh: University of Pittsburgh, Learning Research and Development Center.

Manna, Paul. 2004. "Leaving No Child Behind." In *Political Education: National Policy Comes of Age,* edited by Christopher T. Cross. New York: Teachers College Press.

Maranto, Robert, and April Gresham Maranto. 2004. "Options for Low-Income Students: Evidence from the States." In *Leaving No Child Behind? Options for Kids in Failing Schools,* edited by Frederick M. Hess and Chester E. Finn Jr. New York: Palgrave Macmillan.

McAdams, Donald, Michelle Wisdom, Sarah Glover, and Anne McClellan. 2003. *Urban School District Accountability Systems.* Denver: Education Commission of the States and the Center for Reform of School Systems.

McDonnell, Lorraine. 2004. *Politics, Persuasion, and Educational Testing.* Cambridge: Harvard University Press.

Meier, Deborah. 2000. "Educating a Democracy." In *Will Standards Save Public Education?* edited by Joshua Cohen and Joel Rogers. Boston: Beacon.

———. 2004. "NCLB and Democracy." In *Many Children Left Behind: How the No Child Left Behind Act Is Damaging Our Children and Our Schools,* edited by Deborah Meier and George Wood. Boston: Beacon.

Meier, Deborah, and George Wood, eds. 2004. *Many Children Left Behind: How the No Child Left Behind Act Is Damaging Our Children and Our Schools.* Boston: Beacon.

Meyer, Robert H. 1997. "Value-Added Indicators of School Performance: A Primer." *Economics of Education Review* 16 (3): 283–301.

———. 2002. "Value-Added Indicators: Do They Make a Difference? Evidence from the Milwaukee Public Schools." Paper presented at the annual meeting of the American Educational Research Association, New Orleans, April 2.

Minneapolis Public Schools. 2004. "School Information Report." Available at http://www.incschools.com/mpls/.

Minnesota Department of Education. 2003a. "2003 NCLB Adequate Yearly Progress (AYP) System Requirements/Business Rules." Available at http://cfl.state.mn.us/mde/static/003261.pdf.

———. 2003b. "Adequate Yearly Progress Status by Consequence." Available at http://education.state.mn.us/mde/index.html.

———. 2003c. "Fall Populations by School: 2002–03." Available at http://cfl .state.mn.us/mde/static/GEG0203.xls.

———. 2003d. "Gender by Ethnicity by School: 2002–03." Available at http://cfl.state.mn.us/mde/static/GEG0203.xls.

———. 2003e. "Governor Pawlenty Unveils 'Accountability on a Stick'" (press release). August 21.

———. 2003f. "MCA 2003 Grades 3 & 5 Public Schools 5/18/04 Corrected." Available at http://clf.state.mn.us/mde/static/x19_class2003mcapublic.xls.

———. 2004a. "2004 AYP by Consequence." Available at http://cfl.state.mn.us/ mde/static/AYP%20Results%202004%20-%20All%20Schools%20and %20Districts.XLS.

———. 2004b. "2004 Star Ratings." Available at http://cfl.state.mn.us/ mde/static/Star%20 Results%202004%20-%20All%20Schools.XLS.

———. 2004c. "Governor Pawlenty Announces 'Value-Added' Growth Model to Measure Individual Student Progress" (press release). October 13.

———. 2004d. "MCA 2004 Grades 3, 5, & 7 Public Schools." Available at http://cfl.state.mn.us/mde/static/2004%20MCA%203_5_7%20Pub lic%20Schools.xls.

———. 2004e. "No Questions Left Behind: A Comprehensive Guide to Minnesota's Accountability Plan under the No Child Left Behind Act." Available at http://cfl.state.mn.us/mde/static/003326.pdf.

———. 2005. "Governor Pawlenty: Minnesota's Schools Get Even Better" (press release). August 29.

Minnesota Office of Educational Accountability and University of Minnesota College of Education and Human Development. 2002a. "The 'No Child Left Behind Act' and Minnesota's Standards, Assessments, and Accountability." Available at http://education.umn.edu/oea/PDF/02PolicyBrief.pdf.

———. 2002b. "The Minnesota Basic Skills Test: Performance Gaps on the Reading and Mathematics Tests from 1996 to 2001, by Gender, Ethnicity, Limited English Proficiency, Individual Education Plans, and Socio-Economic Status." Available at http://education.umn.edu/oea/PDF/BSTPerf GapsReport.pdf.

Minnesota Office of the Legislative Auditor. 2004. *Evaluation Report: No Child Left Behind.* Report 04-04. St. Paul: Program Evaluation Division.

Miron, Gary, and Christopher Nelson. 2001. *Student Academic Achievement in Charter Schools: What We Know and Why We Know So Little.* Occasional Paper 41.

New York: National Center for the Study of Privatization in Education, Teachers College, Columbia University.

Moe, Terry M. 2003. "Politics, Control, and the Future of School Accountability." In *No Child Left Behind? The Politics and Practice of School Accountability,* edited by Paul E. Peterson and Martin R. West. Washington, DC: Brookings Institution Press.

Monk, David H. 1989. "The Educational Production Function: Its Evolving Role in Policy Analysis." *Educational Evaluation and Policy Analysis* 11 (1): 31–45.

Mortimore, Peter, Pamela Sammons, Louise Stoll, David Lewis, and Russell Ecob. 1988. *School Matters.* Berkeley: University of California Press.

Murnane, Richard J. 1975. *The Impact of School Resources on the Learning of Inner City Children.* Cambridge, MA: Ballinger.

———. 2000. "The Case for Standards." In *Will Standards Save Public Education?* edited by Joshua Cohen and Joel Rogers. Boston: Beacon.

Murphy, Walter. 1964. *Elements of Judicial Strategy.* Chicago: University of Chicago Press.

National Association of Elementary School Principals and National Association of Secondary School Principals. 2003. *K–12 Principals Guide to No Child Left Behind.* Alexandria, VA: Education Research Service.

National Conference of State Legislatures. 2005. *Task Force on No Child Left Behind: Final Report.* Washington, DC: National Conference of State Legislatures.

National Education Association. 2005. "U.S. Education Department Validates NEA's Concerns, Proposes More Flexibility under 'No Child Left Behind'" (press release). November 21.

———. 2006. "More Schools Are Failing NCLB Law's Adequate Yearly Progress Requirements." Available at www.nea.org.

National School Boards Association. 2005. "NSBA's Bill to Improve No Child Left Behind." *Priority Issue,* January. Available at www.nsba.org.

———. 2006. "Education Vital Signs." *American School Board Journal,* February. Available at www.nsba.org.

The No Child Left Behind Act of 2001. Public Law 107-110, January 8, 2002. 115 Stat. 1425.

Novak, John R., and Bruce Fuller. 2003. *Penalizing Diverse Schools? Similar Test Scores, but Different Students, Bring Federal Sanctions.* PACE Policy Brief 03-4. Stanford: Policy Analysis for California Education.

Oakes, Jeannie. 1989. "What Educational Indicators? The Case for Assessing the School Context." *Educational Evaluation and Policy Analysis* 11 (2): 181–99.

Olson, Mancur. 1971. *The Logic of Collective Action: Public Goods and the Theory of Groups.* Cambridge: Harvard University Press.

Packer, Joel. 2004. "No Child Left Behind and Academic Yearly Progress—Fundamental Flaws: A Forecast for Failure." Paper presented at the Center on Education Policy Forum on Ideas to Improve the Accountability Provisions under the No Child Left Behind Act, Washington, DC, July 28.

Payne, Gavin. 2004. "The Implementation of the Accountability Provisions of the No Child Left Behind Act." Paper presented at the Center on Education

Policy Forum on Ideas to Improve the Accountability Provisions under the No Child Left Behind Act, Washington, DC, July 28.

Peterson, Paul E., and Martin R. West, eds. 2003. *No Child Left Behind? The Politics and Practice of School Accountability.* Washington, DC: Brookings Institution Press.

Pierce, Jason. 2003. "Minimum Size of Subgroups for Adequate Yearly Progress (AYP)." *State Notes: Education Commission of the States,* September. Available at www.ecs.org.

Pirsig, Robert M. 1981. *Zen and the Art of Motorcycle Maintenance: An Inquiry into Values.* New York: Bantam.

Pontiac v. Spellings. 2005. 05-CV-71535-DT.

Popham, W. James. 2004. *America's "Failing" Schools: How Parents and Teachers Can Cope with No Child Left Behind.* New York: RoutledgeFalmer.

Porter, Andrew C. 1991. "Creating a System of School Process Indicators." *Educational Evaluation and Policy Analysis* 13 (1): 13–29.

Powers, Alfred, and Howard McKinley Corning, eds. 1937. *History of Education in Portland.* Portland, OR: WPA Adult Education Project.

Prendergast, Canice. 1999. "The Provision of Incentives in Firms." *Journal of Economic Literature* 37 (1): 7–63.

Pressman, Jeffrey L., and Aaron Wildavsky. 1984. *Implementation: How Great Expectations in Washington are Dashed in Oakland.* Berkeley: University of California Press.

Pugmire, Tim. 2003a. "List of Underachieving Schools Shrinks to 144." Minnesota Public Radio, August 14.

———. 2003b. "School Report Cards Out; Available Online." Minnesota Public Radio, August 21.

Putnam, Robert. 1993. *Making Democracy Work: Civic Traditions in Modern Italy.* Princeton: Princeton University Press.

———. 1995. "Bowling Alone: America's Declining Social Capital." *Journal of Democracy* 6 (1): 65–78.

———. 2000. *Bowling Alone: The Collapse and Revival of American Community.* New York: Simon and Schuster.

Resnick, Lauren B., and Megan Williams Hall. 1998. "Learning Organizations for Sustainable Education Reform." *Daedalus* 127 (4): 89–118.

Robson, Britt. 2004. "Built to Fail." *City Pages,* March 10.

Rowan, Brian, Steven T. Bossert, and David C. Dwyer. 1983. "Research on Effective Schools: A Cautionary Note." *Educational Researcher* 12 (4): 24–31.

Rudalevige, Andrew. 2003. "No Child Left Behind: Forging a Congressional Compromise." In *No Child Left Behind? The Politics and Practice of School Accountability,* edited by Paul E. Peterson and Martin R. West. Washington, DC: Brookings Institution Press.

Ryan, James E. 2004. "The Perverse Incentives of the No Child Left Behind Act." *NYU Law Review* 79 (3): 932–89.

San Antonio Independent School District v. Rodriquez. 1973. 411 U.S. 1.

Sanders, William L., and Sandra P. Horn. 1998. "Research Findings from the Tennessee Value-Added Assessment System (TVAAS) Database: Implications for Educational Evaluation and Research." *Journal of Personnel Evaluation in Education* 12 (3): 247–56.

Schneider, Mark, Paul Teske, Christine Roch, and Melissa Marschall. 1997. "Networks to Nowhere: Segregation and Stratification in Networks of Information about Schools." *American Journal of Political Science* 41 (4): 1201–23.

Simon, Herbert A. 1945. *Administrative Behavior.* New York: Free Press.

Stone, Clarence N., Jeffrey R. Henig, Bryan D. Jones, and Carol Pierannunzi. 2001. *Building Civic Capacity: The Politics of Reforming Urban Schools.* Lawrence: University Press of Kansas.

Summers, Anita A., and Barbara L. Wolfe. 1977. "Do Schools Make a Difference?" *American Economic Review* 67 (4): 639–52.

Sunderman, Gail L., and Jimmy Kim. 2004. *Inspiring Vision, Disappointing Results: Four Studies on Implementing the No Child Left Behind Act.* Cambridge: Civil Rights Project, Harvard University.

Tyack, David B. 1974. *The One Best System: A History of American Urban Education.* Cambridge: Harvard University Press.

U.S. Department of Education. 2002. *Fact Sheet on Title I, Part A.* Washington, DC: Planning and Evaluation Service.

———. 2005. "Secretary Spellings Announces Growth Model Pilot, Addresses Chief State School Officers' Annual Policy Forum in Richmond" (press release). November 18.

U.S. General Accounting Office. 1989. *Effective Schools Programs: Their Extent and Characteristics.* GAO-89-132BR. Washington, DC.

———. 2004a. *Unfunded Mandates: Analysis of Reform Act Coverage.* GAO-04-637. Washington, DC: U.S. General Accounting Office.

———. 2004b. *No Child Left Behind Act: Improvements Needed in Education's Process for Tracking States' Implementation of Key Provisions.* GAO-04-734. Washington, DC: U.S. General Accounting Office.

U.S. Department of Education, Office of the Undersecretary, Elementary and Secondary Education. 2002. *No Child Left Behind: A Desktop Reference 2002.* Washington, DC: U.S. Department of Education, Office of the Undersecretary, Elementary and Secondary Education.

Vanourek, Gregg. 2005. *State of the Charter Movement 2005.* Washington, DC: Charter School Leadership Council.

Verba, Sidney, Kay Lehman Schlozman, and Henry E. Brady. 1995. *Voice and Equality: Civic Volunteerism in American Politics.* Cambridge: Harvard University Press.

Wascoe, Dan. 2005. "Take Your Children to Work . . . Later." *Minneapolis Star Tribune,* 16 April.

Weber, G. 1971. *Inner-City Children Can Be Taught to Read: Four Successful Schools.* Washington, DC: Council for Basic Education.

West, Martin R., and Paul E. Peterson. 2003. "The Politics and Practice of Accountability." In *No Child Left Behind? The Politics and Practice of School Accountability,* edited by Paul E. Peterson and Martin R. West. Washington, DC: Brookings Institution Press.

Wilson, James Q. 1989. *Bureaucracy: What Government Agencies Do and Why They Do It.* New York: Basic Books.

———. 1993. "The Problem of Defining Agency Success." In *Performance Measures for the Criminal Justice System.* Washington, DC: U.S. Department of Justice, Office of Justice Programs, Bureau of Justice Statistics.

Witte, John F. 2000. *The Market Approach to Education: An Analysis of America's First Voucher Program.* Princeton: Princeton University Press.

Witte, John F., and Daniel J. Walsh. 1990. "A Systematic Test of the Effective Schools Model." *Educational Evaluation and Policy Analysis* 12 (2): 188–212.

Wood, George. 2004. "A View from the Field: NCLB's Effects on Classrooms and Schools." In *Many Children Left Behind: How the No Child Left Behind Act Is Damaging Our Children and Our Schools,* edited by Deborah Meier and George Wood. Boston: Beacon.

Wright, Peter W. D., Pamela Darr Wright, and Suzanne Whitney Heath, eds. 2003. *Wrightslaw No Child Left Behind.* Hartfield, VA: Harbor House Law Press.

Yeow Meng, Thum. 2003. *No Child Left Behind: Methodological Challenges and Recommendations for Measuring Adequate Yearly Progress.* CSE Tech Report 590. Los Angeles: Center for the Study of Evaluation, National Center for Research on Evaluation, Standards, and Student Testing, Graduate School of Education and Information Studies, University of California, Los Angeles.

Index